ISRAEL In The Revelation

by
Elmer A. Josephson

Bible Light International
PO Box 370
Ottawa, Kansas 66067-0370 USA

www.Bible-Light.com

Bible Light International
PO Box 370
Ottawa, Kansas 66067-0370 USA

www.Bible-Light.com

Dedication

To the one God of Abraham, Isaac and Jacob, the Covenant God of Israel, who by his spirit "giveth wisdom, out of whose mouth cometh knowledge and understanding," and The Anointed One, the Lord of Life and Redeemer – be all glory and praise forever and ever.

From the Editor

"Whereby when ye read, ye may understand my knowledge in the mystery of Christ" (Ephesians 3:4).

This is one of five books my husband, Elmer Josephson, wrote during our last residency in Jerusalem. The first printing was accomplished before he departed this life in October 1996. Israel in *The Revelation* is a popular book and now we must print a new edition which is in an improved format and somewhat abridged.

I helped Elmer on the Biblical research for this book and he used some of my findings, however, those familiar with his writing style will recognize it is his. It has always been my job to edit: to try to catch anything that might not be clearly expressed, any grammar and punctuation errors, and to plan the format of the book. But any changes I might make, using my own words and thoughts, were submitted to his approval. He rarely vetoed any. I *was*, after all, his "helper", and we worked together as one. And now, I believe I pretty well know what he would want – in reprinting, or in editing his unprinted manuscripts. Also when an addition or up-dating needs to be made because of present day happenings, I endeavor to tag them as "editor's".

In doing the fine-tooth editing, it is necessary for me to read the manuscript several times – at least five. In so doing I am blessed five-fold! I want to share that blessing with you! I want you to have this book and get its truths deep in your mind as will happen especially when RE-read.

– Chris Josephson

Contents

Dedication iii

From the Editor v

Prologue ix

Preface.. xix

Sign-i-fied 23

"Likenesses" 27

The Church in Ephesus 31

The Church in Smyrna..35

The Church in Pergamos...37

The Church in Thyatira..43

The Church in Sardis 45

The Church in Philadelphia 47

The Laodecean Church 53

The Church in Laodecea – Rejected 63

Thrones of Glory..71

Unsealed & Revealed..79

The Sixth Seal 87

"Winds of Judgment"...95

Sun-Clothed Woman 101

Beastly Blasphemy..111

Harvest Time 113

The Coming New World Order...117

About the Author...125

What is Bible Light? 127

Prologue

"... **John, who bare record of the Word of God, and of the testimony of Jesus Christ and of all things which he saw** [not just heard] ...." (Revelation 1:1-2).Though this is not a comprehensive study of the record which John recorded, we had the privilege of 50 years of carefully studying *The Revelation*, with the help of God's Spirit as we have been given. There are mysteries in the Word of God revealed as we need to know them. As we near the fulfillment of a prophetic event, understanding becomes clearer. God said to Daniel, *"**Shut up the words and seal the book even to the time of the end"*** (Daniel 12:4). All indicates we are at this time now in history.

Let us now look to the Lord to guide us as we read and think on it together. As Daniel asked God for wisdom and found it, so let us ask and expect. Above all, the Spirit-anointed Word must be our lodestar and lodestone for all matters concerning both Heaven and Earth.

The Revelation is the last and closing Book of all directly inspired Holy Scripture. It is the longest and most revealing exposition of the Redeemer-Messiah through whom God reveals Himself to all nations.

During the days of his flesh, he was given the earthly name of ***"Jesus – for he shall save his people from their sins,"*** the Angel Gabriel announced to Miriam (Mary – Matthew 1:21). From the translation of the name in Greek we get the English "Jesus" and sometimes "Joshua" which all stems from the Hebrew, *Yehoshua*, meaning salvation.

Many other individuals have carried His 'earthly' name. In

fact, I remember as a boy in Kansas City, Missouri (where I was born and spent my formative years) I knew a dear, mild-mannered Mexican man, who picked up our trash; his name was "Jesus." From the same root we get the word "salvage." We could carry this thought further with the illustration of our trash service man, "Jesus." Our Lord Jesus Christ is in the "salvage" business as He seeks the lost – the cast offs – and they become reborn (not just recycled!) but *"if any man be in Christ, he is a new creation: Old things are passed away; behold all things become new"* (II Corinthians 5:17).

Keep in mind, *"Christ"* is not a name, but a title which means *The Anointed One*. God gave him this title officially at His baptism when God's Spirit came upon Him. In Hebrew, it is *Me-SHEE-ach*[1] – *Messiah*. In Greek, it is *Christos* and in English, *Christ*. This anointing ended 30 years of silence during which there was not one miracle.

Israel is not to be 'dumped' in with other nations in God's dealings. King Balak, the king of Moab, must have learned this after he said to Balaam, *"... Come, curse me Jacob, and come, defy Israel."* Balaam answered, *"How shall I curse, whom God hath not cursed? or how shall I defy, whom the Lord hath not defied? For from the top of the rocks I see him, and from the hills I behold him: lo, the people* [Israel] *shall dwell alone, and shall not be reckoned among the nations"* (Numbers 23:7c-9).

A Personal & Lasting Revelation Experience

Some have said, "I'm not interested in prophecy" – which *The Revelation* is, and very difficult! However, consider: in the beginning of recorded history, practically all Scripture was prophecy. Today most of the Bible is prophecy either fulfilled, unfulfilled or in the process of being fulfilled. In fact, fulfilled prophecy gives the Holy Scriptures its greatest validity and is

---

1   Transliteration from a language such as Hebrew, which has an entirely different alphabet (and without vowels) is usually done however it sounds to the ears of the translator. Hence, the many differences in spellings.

the primary proof of the Bible's divine inspiration.

But in my latter teens, I had probing doubts about the existence of God, the authenticity of the Bible and the claims of Christ. I was honestly seeking Truth, and I had to get it settled.

We lived in the Roanoke District of Kansas City, Missouri. I decided to drive to Penn Valley Park, just south of the then relatively-new Union Station (Railroad Depot). I liked to go to Penn Valley alone, at night (unsafe now!), get out under the stars and try to settle my problems. Kansas City was not as crowded as it is now. It did not have the carbon monoxide gas problem defiling the atmosphere and dulling the vision of the stars in the heavens. There was a favorite spot, high on a hill, I loved to visit.

I laid down on the soft turf to meditate. I looked into the beautifully star-studded heavens and thought, "I'm on one of those stars." I felt as if I were drifting out into space. "How far can one go? If, after billions of light years, you come to a wall, why is it there? And how much farther? to what? There is no end to space!"

Then I thought of time. With God there is no beginning or ending of time. *"Even from everlasting to everlasting thou art God"* (Psalm 90:2). When the LORD God announced by His Mighty Angel (Christ) **'there should be time no longer'** (Revelation 10:6), He was speaking concerning the earth and the seven seas that covers of the earth's surface – *"and the things which are therein."*

These two varieties can 'blow your mind' if you really dwell on them: (1) no end to time, (2) no end to space. Our scientists have built huge telescopes and sent probes into space which pierce out into billions of light years and have seen no sign of any kind of "wall." If there were one – what's on the other side of the wall? More space and billions of universes?

But these two things were not what settled the matter with me.

I had some knowledge of God. I had read the Scriptures through – raggedly. I had read the story of creation. It made far more sense than believing the nebulous fairy-tale theory (an "idea") of evolution (a guess, a supposition).

But as I lay there in Penn Valley Park, I wanted some solid truth upon which to rest.

Then it came:

The Cradle of World Redemption

I had read of Abraham and his descendants in the Bible. Paul, the greatest of the New Testament apostles, calls Abraham, *"the father of us all."* I knew he was the father of the Hebrew people, but how did he become "the father of us" former pagan Gentiles? In two ways: (1) All writers of both the Old and New Testaments were penned by Abraham's Hebrew descendants – "his seed" – family tree through Isaac and Jacob. (2) And the true Christ and Savior of the Nations, *"took not on him the nature of angels, but he took on him the seed of Abraham"* (Hebrews 2:16). *"And if ye be Christ's, then are ye Abraham's seed, and heirs according to the promise"* (Galatians 3:29).

For 2,126 years before Christ, the only ones who knew the true living God of the Universe were the sons and daughters of Abraham. If any Gentile wanted to know the true God or hear anything about Him, they had to go to a Jewish synagogue or talk to a rabbi learned in God's Word. God had made an everlasting covenant (contract) with them. It is found in the Book of Genesis. The preamble (Genesis 12:1-3) reads: *"Now the Lord had said* [about 15 years before] *unto Abram, Get thee out of thy country, and from thy kindred, and from thy father's house, unto a land that I will show thee."*

Then God gave seven brief concise promises:
1) *"And I will make of thee a great nation,*
2) *"And I will bless thee,*
3) *"And make thy name great;*
4) *"And thou shalt be a blessing* [not a curse as Hitler and his Nazi cohorts, attempted to foster on the world.]
5) *"And I will bless them that bless thee, and*
6) *"Curse him that curseth thee:"* Because of promise #4, God gave promises #5 and #6, 'double-indemnity in-

surance clauses.' God is the only One who can write a Health, Life or any such "insurance policy". Earth-born insurance companies can only write "sick" and "death" insurance.

7) *"And in thee shall all families of the earth be blessed"* – the greatest promise of all.

The Eternal wrote and ratified this insurance – and assurance – policy Himself. He gave the ramifications clearly in Genesis 17:1-21. In 21 short verses, the Lord states three times this is *God's EVERLASTING covenant,* a contract with Abraham and his seed. God's *EVERLASTING(s)* in the First ("Old") Testament are as unendingly everlasting as in the "New" Testament when He turned to us former pagan Gentiles through Christ with *"everlasting life."*

We Gentiles were without a covenant, without a promise, without hope and without God in the world. But, we were included in the last promise of the everlasting Abrahamic Covenant when God said to Abraham, *"In thee* [i.e., his seed – family tree] *shall ALL the nations of the earth be blessed."* How could this be?

Read slowly and don't twist or be twisted.

"Now to Abraham and his seed [family tree] *were the promises made. He saith not, And to seeds, as of many;* [other family trees such as Ishmael's, Esau's and the sons of Keturah, whom Abraham married after the death of Sarah. These became the progenitors of the Arab peoples.] *but as of one* [the one 'tree' of Isaac, Jacob and the 12 tribes]. *AND* [in addition] *to thy seed, which is Christ* [The Anointed One]. *And this I say, that the covenant, that was confirmed before of God in Christ, the law, which was four hundred and thirty years after, cannot disannual, that it should make the promise of none effect.*

"For if the inheritance be of the law, it is no more of promise: but God gave it to Abraham by promise" (Galatians 3:16-18).

That night in the park under the stars, I thought further: Every Book in the Book of God, both the so-called "Old" (the first) Testament and the "New" Testament was penned by a son of Abraham. Christ through whom God turned to us Gentiles, therefore, had to be born of Abraham's seed (family tree) according to God's promise to Abraham, *"the father of us all,"* as Paul declared. ***"And if ye be Christ's then are ye Abraham's seed and heirs according to the promise"*** (Galatians 3:29).

As I lay there wondering and pondering on what I'd read in the Bible and had experienced among people, one great deciding factor and stabilizing truth began to emerge. Of course, I had no idea of what I would learn in the next 50 years, but the following thoughts came.

In Summary

Here is a great segment of people still in the world that has had an eternal attachment to the Almighty for over 4,000 years; 2,126 years before their Messiah's appearance as Jesus. The Creator chooses to call Himself by their name, ***"THE GOD OF ISRAEL,"*** scores of times, more than by any other name. These descendants of Abraham – which have come to be called "Jews" – have maintained their identity as a solid, God-fearing, righteous people. They have contributed much in many areas of life wherever they have lived.[2]

These are not perfect, yet their homes, overall, are more intact than any other ethnic group including so called Christian – yes, "even" evangelicals. For the most part, God has not given them to believe that Christ was the Messiah. It's no wonder when He is so grossly misrepresented in hundreds of different "likenesses," made contrary to God's Word (Exodus 20:4-6). And considering also the atrocious treatment of Jews by "Christians" in the Spanish Inquisition, the Crusades, etc. (We put quotation marks around "Christian" because the true meaning is "a follower of Christ" – and such actions certainly do not emulate Him!)

---

2   We suggest a careful reading of ***Israel, God's Key to World Redemption***, still available at Bible Light Publications, PO Box 370, Ottawa, KS 66067 or online from www.Bible-Light.com.

Further, if all the people of Israel had accepted Christ when He came the first time, they would have come out of the synagogues and their Judaic heritage, and intermarried among all the Gentile nations. They would have been swallowed up among and by the nations – to their total destruction, so that in a few generations there would have been no Jews left on the face of the earth. (This is what Russia attempted to do, but we have seen God's hand in their rescue.) Christians who proselytize do the same, under guise of 'saving' God's chosen people from hell, and cause Jewish intermarriage with Gentiles. In order to protect His people from being annihilated through intermarriage, and to preserve Israel intact for Messiah's glorious revelation, He issued the physical death penalty for such 'conversion.' This is why today, though the death penalty is not imposed on Jews for converting, they are sometimes treated as "dead" by the family.

Consider

If this people were wiped out, it would make God a liar, His Book untrustworthy and unreliable fairy tales and fables. Why? They had to fulfill God's promise to Abraham: Genesis 12:1-3; 17:1-21. Ignorant Gentiles make light of this to their own destruction: *"I will curse him that curseth thee"* – that is, have any part in their annihilation, which happens in intermarriage into Gentile 'religions' – regardless how 'wellmeaning.'

God clearly promised: *"Thus saith the LORD, which giveth the sun for a light by day, and the ordinances of the moon and of the stars for a light by night, which divideth the sea when the waves thereof roar: The Lord of hosts is his name: If those ordinance* [sun, moon, and stars] *depart from before me, saith the LORD, then the seed* [family tree, descendants] *of Israel also shall cease from being a nation before Me for ever."*

Think on this: *"Thus saith the LORD: If heaven above can be measured, and the foundations of the earth searched out* [then] *I will also cast off all the seed of Israel for all that they have done, saith the LORD"* (Jeremiah 31:35-37).

Why all this introduction to this book, "Israel in the Revelation"? Because it is this people with whom we are deeply involved, because *"Salvation is of the Jews"* (John 4:24). Jesus was saying, *'this is the most important matter in this world and effects the world to come.'* Without this background of Biblical history, the truth we have to present would be like trying to build a house without a foundation, to grow a tree without roots, to have a baby born without a mother and like saying, "have a beautiful day," without the light of the sun – or the moon or the stars!

As I considered these historic and Scriptural facts, my faith in the God of Israel settled firmly on this foundation stone. As a young man, it settled matters in my mind and started me on my life work in the ministry of God's Word – His unfailing Truth. I realized I could fully depend on the God of Israel.

A Further Introductory "Word"

It must be noted – John, the beloved disciple, was the (human) author of the Gospel by his name and the epistles of I, II, and III John as well as *The Revelation*. God gave him the WORLD vision in his books. The other N.T. books have a sprinkling of the word, "world". John mentions it a total of 84 times in his. John presents Christ to the world – the nations.

"He was in the world, and the world was made by him, and the world knew him not" (John 1:10). He gave the world (nations) the golden text of the Bible – John 3:16. God chose John to seal the canon of all Holy Writ.

It is John that reveals Christ as **"the Lamb slain from the foundation of the world"** (Revelation 13:8).

Read II Timothy 1:9-10; I Peter 1:18-21 and Ephesians 1:4 to corroborate and be blessed. And John was chosen of God to give the world the last words of Christ and offer the final invitation to drink of the water of life freely (Revelation 22:17).

In *The Revelation*, the Spirit of God commissions John to the responsibility of announcing the awesome final warning in

Christ's last words to those who trifle with God's Word. This is far worse than the physical death penalty given under the Law God gave Moses on Mt. Sinai (Revelation 22:18,19).

"For I testify unto every man that heareth the words of the prophecy of this book, If any man shall add unto these, God shall add unto him the plagues that are written in this book: And if any man shall take away from the words of the book of this prophecy, God shall take away his part out of the book of life, and out of the holy city, and from the things which are written in this book" (Revelation 22:18,19).

Preface

"Blessed is he that readeth, and they that hear the words of this prophecy, and keep those things which are written therein: for the time is at hand" (Revelation 1:3).

The Revelation is the only Book in the Bible that begins with a special blessing promised to the reader who <u>hears</u> the words and keeps (observes) them – no doubt because it seems difficult to read and comprehend.

I recall my <u>first</u> visit to the Middle East in 1960. I traveled alone. (Since then we have lived an aggregate of eight years there and during four Mideast Wars.) I had flown to Beirut, Lebanon from Cairo, Egypt, the night before. The next morning, I opened the door to the balcony of my room atop the hotel overlooking the Mediterranean Sea. I automatically gasped aloud, *"WHAT A GORGEOUS view."* Then I was jerked fully awake and realized no one else was around.

Never was the vast Mediterranean Sea more blue and beautiful. A perfect balmy breeze was blowing large waves with white caps that were breaking on the rocky shore below. Immediately to the south stretched the shoreline toward the mountains of Northern Israel, including Mt. Carmel at Haifa where Elijah challenged King Ahab about his turning away from the God of Israel to the false prophets of Baal. (Recorded in I Kings 18. Read it and be refreshed. Remember, He is the same God today.)

I thought, *"Soon I will be in that land I have read about all my life."* But I still had a schedule of two days in Lebanon, two days in Syria, and four days in 'Jordan'. And it was like coming home to arrive in Israel. What a contrast from traveling in 22 other lands that are mostly stagnant: no immigration; cultures dead in comparison. There was a sense of the presence of God, in the Land of Israel and among His "chosen people." This 4,000 year old nation and land was vibrant after being reborn in our generation. Each day witnessed new immigrants, new industry, great building programs.

A Sideline Personal Interest Story

Back in Beirut, Lebanon, that morning when I went down for breakfast, I had an experience that struck and stuck with me. I was sitting alone looking over the menu between glimpses of the morning news. A man from London was sitting at a table next to me also reading the morning paper. The waitress asked him a question. After a pause, he suddenly said, *"I'm sorry, I was only listening with half an ear."* I had never heard that expression before.

It stuck, and I thought, *"How many listen to the most important, the greatest masterpiece of Holy Writ in the world with 'half an ear'?"* We're not so much heavenly minded that we're of no earthly use, as we are so earthly minded we are of no heavenly use! We are tuned to earthy noises rather than His voice from heaven because of the louder clatter of perishables.

The Last Shall be First

All believers should be vitally concerned about this last Book of the Bible – *The Revelation*. Genesis, the first Book, means and marks the *beginning*. In it is revealed a detailed account how God's creative wonders began: the heaven, the sun, moon, and stars. And the magnificent WORD gave them their start. Think of the earth, the seven seas and all in them, the plants and trees, the thousands of species of birds and animals, and God's crowning creation – mankind and nations – and then chief of these nations, Israel, for *"In thee shall all the nations of the earth be blessed."*

This is why

When we open the New Testament (where God in His mercy turned to the pagan Gentile nations) we read:

"The book of the generations of Jesus Christ, the son of David, the son of Abraham. Abraham begat Isaac; and Isaac

begat Jacob; and Jacob begat Judah and his brethren...."

Then starts the 2,126 years B.C. genealogy from Abraham to the birth of Christ. This marked the beginning of the fulfillment of God's promise to Abraham, *"In thee* [Abraham and his family tree, Israel] *shall all the nations of the earth be blessed."*

This is the reason also why we read so much concerning Israel in a positive vein in this last of the divinely inspired Books of the Bible.

"The Revelation" means what its name implies. In it the Lord *revealed* what was just ahead from that date, 96 A.D., to the true Messiah's on-planet-earth's appearance and into His reign in Jerusalem over Israel and the whole earth.

After this reign of the true Messiah on the earth, there are glimpses into the eternity beyond, as the Apostle Paul writes:

"Then cometh the end, when he shall have delivered up the kingdom to God, even the Father; when he shall have put down all rule and all authority and power. For he must reign, till he hath put all enemies under his feet. The last enemy that shall be destroyed is death. For he hath put all things under his feet. But when he said, all things are put under him, it is manifest that he is excepted, which did put all things under him. And when all things shall be subdued unto him, then shall the Son also himself be subject unto him that put all things under him, that God may be all in all" (I Corinthians 15:24-28).

Recall, the writer of *The Revelation* is the beloved Apostle John, who lived to be 115 years of age. He was writing as a prisoner of Rome, exiled to this lonely isle of Patmos (Revelation 1:9) off the west coast of Turkey, then Asia Minor. Why? **"For the word of God, and for the testimony of Jesus Christ."**

The only Bible the early church had for 300 years was the First Testament – the Hebrew Scriptures, so-called "Old" Testament. Our present New Testament, of Paul's letters and various writings floating around among the churches, were not assembled and verified until the Council of Carthage in 397 A.D.

In our day, it has been torn to shreds in hundreds of so-called translations which are mostly private interpretations and paraphrases – and which have made their "producers" rich in mannon – but that's another volumn!

Please read carefully this great and last Book of Heaven's Library – *The Revelation*. Let us ask God's Spirit to open our hearts to His Word – and hear *"all that is written therein"*. When God promises, He means it! And fulfills ALL He has written.

So come along, let's read and be blessed together. Let us begin the Biblical journey, a look into the future and God's eternal plans and perfect purposes for His people.

(All Scripture quotations in this book are from the King James version, unless otherwise specified. Scripture quotes from the Book of **The Revelation** are in bold; the italic are other Scripture quotes. Our comments within a Bible quote are in brackets and normal type.)

Sign-i-fied

The Revelation, Chapter 1

In order to properly understand this last Book of the Bible, called, *"The Revelation"* we must use and not lose the Key. It unlocks all its treasures.

V. 1, **"The Revelation of Jesus Christ, which God gave unto him** [Christ]**, to show unto his servants things which must shortly come to pass; and he sent and signified it by his** [God's] **angel** [Messenger – Christ] **unto his servant John."** He (Christ) will show (not hide) but reveal unto His servants (those who are His ministers) things which are due to start happening immediately: and,

"He [God] **sent and SIGNIFIED...."** Breaking down the word, it is *sign-i-fied*. That is, it was to be given in *signs, symbols, figures*.

The Revelation is not to be taken literally; to do so causes a wilderness of confusion.

Channel of Light

As we shall soon see: "the sun" is a type of Israel through whom all the light of God has come.

Physically all the light we have on earth, the warmth, energy that sustains all life comes from the sun. We are held in orbit by the sun's pull as though an eleven-inch steel cable were attached to every foot of the earth surface.

"Thy Word is a lamp to my feet a light unto a path" (Psalm 119:105).

Every penman of the Book of God is an Israelite. Christ who was born of the seed of Abraham (Hebrews 2:16) said, *"I am the light of the world: he that followeth me shall not walk in darkness, but shall have the light of life"* (John 8:12).

Note carefully how this Revelation comes down to us: The Father gave it to the Son and then sent Him (Christ) to give it to John. "Christ" – "Angel" [Messenger] is one and the same. It is "shown" – revealed – unto "his servants" – bond-slaves who must be yielded to the Master to understand this Revelation.

V. 2, **"Who bare record of the Word of God, and of the testimony of Jesus Christ, and of all things that he** [John] **saw."**

In *The Revelation*, John records that he "saw", 39 times with the closing oath, **"I, John saw these things and heard."** He used the term, "heard", 33 times. Who dares doubt the beloved disciple whom God gave 115 years of life on this planet?

The key to the code and the order of witness is:

First, the Word of God; second, the Testimony of Christ; third, the things which John saw.

To understand the Book, look for the meaning behind the symbols. To reiterate: Do not take *The Revelation* literally.

Results Can Be Expected

V. 3, **"Blessed** [happy, enriched] **is he that readeth, and they that hear the words of this prophecy, and keep** [observe] **those things which are written therein: for the time is at hand."**

The Revelation is the only Book in all the Bible that promises a special incentive to read and special blessing to those who do read and 'hear' (with open inner ear) this prophecy, and who observe and act upon it. Results can be expected.

In the early days of the Bible, it all was inscribed on hand-written scrolls. Very few had the privilege of reading it. The scrolls were very expensive, almost priceless. There was no New Testament as we have it today until the fourth century when the list of 27 books were finally agreed upon as canonical.

This meant that the early Church had the First Testament only, the so-called "Old Testament," i.e., the Hebrew Scriptures, as their total, complete, authentic Holy Scriptures. It was written in the Hebrew language which only the educated Hebrew people, as the scribes and rabbis, could read and understand. (There was also a Greek translation called the "Septuagint.")

God inspired 'John-the-Revelator' to give this special blessing of encouragement for ALL to read. It first refers to those who can read, secondly to those who will hear and believe – and above all, who will observe and follow.

"Likenesses"

Our subject is *Israel in The Revelation*. The theme of the entire book of *The Revelation* is the Messiah of Israel. Let us read the initial vision of Him given to John at the time of:
The Revelation 1:13-16:

"... And in the midst of the seven candlesticks one like unto the Son of man, clothed with a garment down to the foot, and girt about the paps with a golden girdle.

"His head and his hairs were white like wool, as white as snow; and his eyes were as a flame of fire;

"And his feet like unto fine brass, as if they burned in a furnace; and his voice as the sound of many waters.

"And he had in his right hand seven stars: and out of his mouth went a sharp two edged sword: and his countenance was as the sun shineth in his strength."

This vision is a far cry from the physical faces pictured in stained glass windows, in Bibles and Christian literature galore – not to mention the "pictures" of Christ sold over the counter for money of all denominations.

Those "likenesses" God's Word forbids

Christ warned, ***"Many shall come in my name, saying, I am Christ*** [which in essence is over every picture]***; and shall deceive many"*** (Matthew 24:5 & Mark 13:6). We tell our little children as we show them these pictures conjured up in minds of artists, *"This is Jesus Christ."* It looks like a Gentile with long hair!

Being born of a 100% Jewish mother, a legal Jewish father, Jesus should appear as the most authentic, glorified Jewish Rabbi ever! But it is forbidden to try to picture Him, even thus.

"Thou shalt not make unto thee any graven image, or any likeness of any thing that is in heaven above, or that is in the earth beneath, or that is in the water under the earth:

"Thou shalt not bow down thyself to them, nor serve them...." (Exodus 20:4,5).

We DO bow down to and serve Christ; therefore, to make an image or likeness of Him now is forbidden. Yes, He surely did become a man and *"took on Him the seed of Abraham"* (Hebrews 2:16), but the Apostle Paul admonishes, *"Though we have known Christ after the flesh, yet now henceforth know we him no more"* (II Corinthians 5:16) – that is, we cannot localize Him to a man in a body. He will appear again in that form during the Kingdom Age to carry out His kingdom duties; above all, however, He is Spirit: *"Now the Lord is that Spirit and where the Spirit of the Lord is, there is liberty"* (II Corinthians 3:17).

Suppose you were moving to a newly founded city to be the town's doctor. They were going to have a great big celebration at your arrival. Since your name was quite common, people from all over the area sent in different pictures and photos of a person who had your name, thinking it was their special friend. These copies of all kinds of pictures were circulated about town. When you got there, confusion reigned and few recognized you.

This is not one scintilla of the confusion we are making of Christ by the hundreds and thousands of so-called "pictures of Jesus." After His resurrection and ascension, the only picture we have is that which Saul of Tarsus (later Paul) and John the Revelator saw: His face was as the brightness of the sun shining in its full strength. If we want an image now, we can go out and look at the sun in its noonday strength! (But don't try it; you can damage your eyes.)

Paul says, He *"is the image of the INVISIBLE GOD"* – and we are forbidden in God's word to make a *"likeness."*

God has appointed Christ to be the Executive Director of the Universe: *"All power is GIVEN unto me in heaven and in earth"* (Matthew 28:18). God has given unto Him the authority to execute judgment for He *"hath committed all judgment to the Son"* (John 5:22). This is what the Book of *The Revelation* is all about.

Why should we seek to picture Him now as a man? To pull Him down to our level? No wonder He is not taken seriously enough by the world at large.

Why all this in a volume titled, *"Israel in The Revelation"*? Because the church's roots are in the Hebrew Scriptures that forbids any **"likeness."** Our pictures and statues of Jesus are not only a stumbling block and an abomination to our Jewish brethren, they are actually forbidden also in the N.T. scriptures!

At the beginning of each of the 7 messages given to the churches (7 ages of church history) in *The Revelation*, is a description of Christ. Let's discover – and recover – THESE!

The Church in Ephesus
The Revelation, Chapter 2

"These things saith He that holdeth the seven stars in His right hand, who walketh in the midst...." (V. 1)

V. 2, **"I know thy works ... thou hast tried them which say they are apostles, and are not, and hast found them liars"** – as in the case of Ananias and Sapphira, his wife. (Read Acts 5:1-11.)

Although the seven churches of Asia were actual assemblies of believers whom the Book of *The Revelation* addressed, they also depict church ages. Elements of each age are still with us today, but there are distinctions that appertain – and originate – in each age. These lace the accepted doctrinal teachings of following ages – whether right or wrong.

In this volume, we seek to confine our study to only those elementary doctrines as they pertain to Israel and the Jewish nation.

"Rejection" is a favorite word in Christendom in referring to Israel. What is meant by the word is: "God has rejected them because they rejected Jesus." However, we have grossly erred in that a large segment of the church has rejected foundational truths in the Hebrew Scriptures. We have departed so far from our roots that we 'boast against the branches.' **"But if thou boast, thou bearest not the root, but the root thee"** (Romans 11:18).

The last (Laodicean) Church-Age is corrupt and in many ways *Apostate*. The two words, *apostolic* and *apostate*, are similar in sound but are opposite in meaning. While *apostolic* means *as the Apostles*, i.e., sent ones, *apostate* means *departure from the teachings of Christ and His Apostles.*

The apostasy began very early in the Gentile Church, as we shall see in the progress of this study of *Israel in The Revelation.*

However, in the FIRST Church age (the Ephesian) the apostacy was soon exposed and quickly judged. This LAST Church Age (the Laodicean) smug and unrepentant, awaits the fearsome *"Judgment Seat of Christ."* Paul warns believers, *"knowing therefore the terror of the Lord, we persuade* [prepare] *men"* (II Corinthians 5:10-11).

V.4, **"Nevertheless I have *somewhat* against thee, because thou hast left thy first love."**

What was 'their first love'?

Consider how these Gentiles at Ephesus must have felt when the Gospel was preached to them. Read the major happenings at Ephesus in Acts 19.

Paul stayed on two full years in Ephesus, preaching: ***"the Gospel of your salvation.... Wherefore remember, that ye being in time past Gentiles in the flesh, who are called Uncircumcision by that which is called the Circumcision in the flesh made by hands; That at that time ye were without Christ, being aliens from the commonwealth of Israel, and strangers from the covenants of promise, having no hope, and without God in the world:***

"But now in Christ Jesus ye who sometimes were far off are made nigh by the blood of Christ" (Ephesians 1:13, 2:11-13). Read the full book of Ephesians to get an understanding of the maturity of these believers and a further study of the *far off* and *nigh* ones. (Read especially V. 17 of Ephesians 2, Zechariah 6:15; Acts 2:39; and our book: ***Israel, God's Key to World Redemption***, Chapter 21.)

What was their "First Love"? The realization that through Christ, the Gentiles also were brought into the household of Abraham, but not to the exclusion of Abraham's house! NOT at the eternal expense of driving Israel out of her own house as the foolish and diabolical replacement theology teaches, i.e., *"Only the Church now is Israel; and the Jews are rejected by God."*

How error begins

Losing this truth cut **roots** and severed Gentiles from Jews; thus began the apostacy and deterioration of the church. By cutting away and severing also the Hebrew Scriptures, they came to be called "OLD Testament – those Jewish Laws," etc.

The Apostle Paul – called the giant of the New Testament – clearly warned of the apostacy. Please read and meditate on the whole chapter of Romans 11 in light of our subject. Thus the Apostacy had already begun in Ephesus – the first Church Age!

Israel's election is by virtue of the **Everlasting** Abrahamic Covenant. Losing this truth was the result of overemphasis on some of Paul's teaching without carefully considering ALL he said on the subject, and by taking it out of context.

This is always how error begins. For instance, it has happened sometimes to Galatians 3:29, ***"And if ye be Christ's, then are ye Abraham's seed, and heirs according to the promise."***

The primarily all-Gentile Church became self-contained, not only forgetting the pit from which they (and we), as pagans, had been dug, but the true olive tree, Israel, into which they/we were grafted (Romans 11:24-27). This **tree of life** truth will crop up again when we consider verse 7.

V. 6, **"But this thou hast, that thou hatest the deeds of the Nicolaitans, which I also hate."**

The Nicolaitans were a sect which taught freedom to act and eat as heathen, including poisonous, unclean, flesh-eating animals contrary to Acts 15:29.

"Freedom of the flesh" teaching is again tantamount and rampant today! It continually reoccurs and defiles the Body of Believers. (More about this in the Pergamos Church, Vs. 14, 15 & 20 and Chapter 5 of this volume.)

Born of Gentile conceit against which Paul so clearly warned, the Nicolaitan doctrine is foundational to what is known today as *Replacement Theology* – i.e., "WE, the Church, are the only people of God now. WE are Israel."

V. 7, **"He that hath an ear, let him hear what the Spirit saith unto the churches. To him that overcometh[3] will I give to eat of <u>the tree of life</u>, which is in <u>the midst</u> of the paradise of God."**

What is "the tree of life?"

"My son, forget not my law ... Happy is the man that findeth wisdom, and the man that getteth understanding ... She is a tree of life to them that lay hold upon her: and happy is every one that retaineth her...." (Proverbs 3:1, 13 & 18).

Again in Proverbs 11:30: *"The fruit of the righteous is a tree of life ..."*

The "tree of life" is the wisdom and righteousness of God which is revealed in and by God's eternal Law.

Christ said, *"It is the spirit that quickeneth; the flesh profiteth nothing: the WORDS that I speak unto you, they are spirit, and they are life"* (John 6:63; see also Deuteronomy 8:3 and Matthew 4:4).

Note that the tree of life here in our study of *The Revelation* is in the *midst* of the paradise of God. That means it is *central*.

It is this center-stage truth of God, personified in Israel, that our "carnal nature" rebels against – that is, His righteous and holy Law. Satan, the world and the evil nature of mankind is a trinity that hates Israel for giving us all the light and knowledge of God we have through His Word and by the Redeemer.

The seed of this movement began as the Ephesian Church 'lost her first love' and thereby became entrenched early in the history of the Second Church Age which we will consider in the next chapter.

---

3   The word "overcometh" carries many aspects of defeating the "freedom" transgression. In this place, the chief culprit is Gentile pride and conceit against Israel.

The Church in Smyrna
The Revelation, Chapter 2 continued

"**And to the angel** [messenger, pastor] **of the church in Smyrna write; These things saith the first and the last, which was dead, and is alive**" (V. 8).

Christ is speaking and He says:

V. 9, "**I know thy works, and tribulation, and poverty, (but thou art rich) and *I know* the blasphemy of them which say they are Jews, and are not, but *are* the synagogue** [assembly] **of Satan.**"

Christ rebukes those who say they are Jews and are not. In the Greek, the word translated "synagogue" and "church" merely means "assembly." In this instance, the translation should not be synagogue, but "**the assembly of Satan.**"

Why is it that so often when the text is favorable, the Christian editors translate it "church" – and when it is judgment and rebuke, they choose "synagogue"? The Greek denotes an assembly of people and could be either Jews or Christians.

So this false teaching that spread throughout Europe and now America was prevalent already in the second church age saying, *We are the real Jews.* One branch calls themselves, *British Israel* and another *Anglo-Israel.* And the latest pursuit among Christians having a love for israel is to discover *OUR Jewish roots* – meaning *"We are of Ephriam – a lost tribe being discovered"*[4]

---

4   There is a genuine pursuit of "our Jewish roots" which seeks to restore to the Church our Spiritual heritage. We take issue with the element that seeks to make Gentiles replace Israel in any way. Some are seeking to do this even in the physical sense. This is expressed as "I've as much right to the Land [of Israel] as the Jews."

Satanic forces continually play on the Gentile Conceit Paul so explicitly warns against.

"The Lord knoweth them that are his" (II Timothy 2:19). It is enough to say, these who teach such perversion do not have the *seal* of the Everlasting Abrahamic Covenant.

Circumcision

God's Covenant relationship with Israel is very clear in its operation, its sign, token and seal, as distinctly set forth in the ratification and ramifications of the Everlasting Abrahamic Covenant, precisely outlined in Genesis 17:1-21.

We have written on this in the book *Israel, God's Key to World Redemption* and will not take time to repeat it here; however, it's indelibly clear that Hitler and the Nazis, who were dripping with hatred, scorn and indignities, knew exactly who the Jews were! They didn't go after the Christian, even those who claimed they were "spiritual Israel."

The Lord God of the Universe has the prerogative and sole rights to place His divine mark upon His people as His sign, token and seal of ownership. He clearly states this in Genesis 17: *"And ye shall circumcise the flesh of your foreskin; and it shall be a TOKEN of the covenant* [contract] *betwixt me and you.*

"And he that is eight days old shall be circumcised among you ... And my covenant shall be in your flesh for an everlasting covenant.

"And the uncircumcised man child whose flesh of his foreskin is not circumcised, that soul shall be cut off from his people; he hath broken my covenant" (Vs. 11-14).

The message to the church in Smyrna concludes with:

V. 10, **"Fear none of those things ... be thou faithful unto death, and I will give thee a crown of life."**

The Church in Pergamos
The Revelation, Chapter 2 continued

"**These things saith He which hath the sharp sword with two edges**" (2:12).

"Pergamos" means "citadel". Satanic blinding and binding forces in the early institutional church structure warred against and sought to invade the "Citadel," the fortress, the refuge believers have in God.

V.13, "**I know thy works, and where thou dwellest, even where Satan's seat is: and thou holdest fast my name, and hath not denied my faith, even in those days wherein Antipas was my faithful martyr, who was slain among you, where Satan dwelleth.**"

What was the first 'crack in the door' which let Satan in? Pride, Gentile conceit beginning in the Ephesian Age and prominent in the Smyrnian Age. Now in the Pergamosian Age the revival of the Doctrine of Balaam, as well.

The-church-is-now-Israel-and-God-is-through-with-the-Jews theology is the cornerstone of anti-Semitism.

Balaam

In Revelation 2:14 the Lord warns against the doctrine of Balaam. Read the whole Balaam story in Numbers, chapters 22 through 24: how Balak, the King of Moab, sought to defeat the Children of Israel by hiring the "prophet" Balaam to curse them.

King Balak thought Israel was coming to take over his land. However if Balak had inquired at the right source, he would not have had that worry: ***"The Lord said unto me*** [Moses]***, 'Distress not the Moabites, neither contend with them in battle: for I will not give thee of their land for a possession; because I have given Ar unto the children of Lot for a possession' "*** (Deuteronomy 2:9) – Moab and Ammon were children of Lot's daughters. We would also have a lot less worrying to do if we knew the Word of God, and obeyed it instantly.

King Balak sent a top government committee to persuade Balaam to curse Israel, *"For,"* he said, *"I have noted that whom you curse are cursed and those whom you bless are blessed. Now curse Israel."* Balaam said, *'Let me pray about it tonight and I'll let you know in the morning.'* He prayed and received the answer *"Do not curse Israel for THEY ARE BLESSED."*

The next morning Balaam reported to this committee of Balak and said, *"Go home for the Lord refuses to let me go with you."* But his prejudice and pride wouldn't let him tell them WHY God told him not to go. They returned to Balak and gave the typical media report, ***"Balaam refuses to come with us"*** – leaving God out of the picture!

Then King Balak sent a more influential government delegation to Prophet Balaam with great promises of reward. Balaam said, ***"If Balak would give me his house full of silver and gold, I cannot go beyond the Word of the Lord my God to do less or more."*** Balaam talked like some big, sound fundamental Christian. He professed a lot, but:

Balaam looked at the size of the reward and thought of the popularity and honor, and said, ***'Let me pray more about it and I'll let you know in the morning.'*** The Lord got disgusted with Balaam and said, *'Go ahead and go with them.'* God sometimes *'gives us our request, but sends leanness of soul'* (Psalm 106:15).

As Balaam was riding his donkey through the narrows with a stone wall on each side, the Lord sent a hindering angel that stopped Balaam's donkey dead in his tracks. Balaam started cursing and blaming his donkey for all of his troubles – a sure sign of not walking with the Lord. He kept beating him. Finally the donkey fell down under him. Balaam began beating him more. Then

God opened the mouth of the donkey – which proves He can use anything He chooses. The donkey said, *'Haven't I been obedient to you all these years and never balked at anything? Why do you treat me like this?'* The donkey had seen the angel, but Balaam's rebellion – love for money and reward, loud profession but total disobedience – had blinded his eyes.

When the Angel of the Lord opened Balaam's eyes, he saw a sword in the hand of the angel who said, **'If the donkey had not turned from me, I would have slain you and saved her.'**

You should read and study the whole account in Numbers 22 through 24. It is a lesson every true believer needs to learn thoroughly, especially those who serve as ministers in any capacity. It is a warning to those who in any wise curse God's chosen people, Israel, through whom God the Almighty has sent all of His Word – and in turning to the Gentiles, God revealed Himself through His Son, Jesus Christ who **"took not on Him the nature of angels, but he took on him the seed of Abraham"** (Hebrews 2:16).

In the tremendous everlasting Abrahamic Covenant, God has put a protective clause: **"I will bless them that bless thee** [Israel] **and I will curse him that curseth thee"** (Genesis 12:3). And there are Christians today who are teaching and preaching that Israel is cursed, calling them "a damned nation."

God gave Balaam to say, **"How shall I curse whom God has not cursed? or how shall I defy whom the Lord hath not defied? For from the top of the rocks I see him, and from the hills I behold him: Lo, the people shall dwell alone AND SHALL NOT BE RECKONED AMONG THE NATIONS"** (Numbers 23:8-9). Yet Christians today still class Israel among the unbelieving and ungodly nations of the earth. Contrariwise, God in the Everlasting Covenant to Abraham and his seed (family tree) declared, **"All the earth is mine and YE** [Israel] **– shall be unto me a kingdom of priests."**

Reminder: (1) Every Word of God, both testaments, has come through Israel. (2) When God turned to the Gentile nations, it was through Jesus Christ who had to be born of the son and seed of Abraham. His virgin mother was "Miriam" of King David's line (See Luke 3 for "Mary's" genealogy.) We need not quote it again, but memorize Hebrews 2:16. So Messiah (The Anointed One) revealed in Jesus said, *"Salvation is of the Jews"* (John 4:22).

How Satan and all his cohorts hate this, try to deny it and more: try to curse Israel. This is often for financial gain – the very "sin" for which they accuse Jews. But it is the curser whom God brings under His curse. Note:

"God is not a man that He should lie; neither the son of man that He should repent; [He will not change his mind about His Everlasting Abrahamic Covenant with Israel] *hath he said, and shall he not do it? or hath he spoken, and shall He not make it good? Behold, I have received commandment to bless: and He hath blessed; and I cannot reverse it.* [Yet a lot of Christians continue to attempt to do this!] *He hath not beheld iniquity in Jacob* [Let us hear this, i.e., we who were former heathen Gentiles – but by God's grace, through Christ, have been brought into the household of Abraham!] *neither hath He seen perverseness in Israel: the LORD his God is with him, and the shout of a king is among them"* (Numbers 23:19-21).

No perverseness? No iniquity? This was during a time many in Israel were committing adultery with the Moabites. God didn't know it? Preposterous – of course He did! Why then did He say this?

> God looks at Israel through the blood atonement and Gentiles cannot curse Israel without getting their "foot crushed against a wall."

"Surely there is no enchantment [no one can put a curse or "hex" on Jacob, whose name was changed to Israel by which they are known now] *neither is there any divination* [regardless how powerful and spiritual any may think they are to perform miracles] *against Israel. According to this time it shall be said of Jacob and of Israel, WHAT HATH GOD WROUGHT!"* (V.

23). Current theological lies even attempt to proclaim, "there are no Jews today." Then who are these 2,000-years preserved and regathering now to the land God promised Abraham, Isaac and Jacob?

This is the warning of Revelation 2:14.

God made it clear to this Gentile Prophet Balaam, but Gentile conceit, pride and outright hatred of God's chosen people opaqued the message and caused Balaam to teach **"Balak to cast a stumbling block before the children of Israel...."**

The doctrine of Balaam and the doctrine of the Nicolaitans go hand in hand: Self promotion, material gain, even denominational insurance companies springing up to "provide and protect," proclaim the doctrine of the Nicolaitans (Vs. 14, 15). The doctrine of Balaam in the church was the mixing of pagan practice with true worship – for gain, graft and politics.

The name "Balaam" also refers to an 'overlord' – which doctrine erupts constantly and upon which cults are built. (The same is true also of "Jezebel" in V. 20.[5])

Alike but Different

Not only is there some overlapping of the church ages, but also in every church age are elements predominate to that particular era. And in each one, the invitation comes to *individuals* in the church:

V. 17, **"He that hath an ear, let him hear what the SPIRIT saith unto the churches; To him that OVERCOMETH will I give to eat of the hidden manna, and will give him a white stone, and in the stone a new name written...."** [Reference to the Talmud/Sand. 106a].

---

5   Note from vs. 14 & 20 the connection between "eating" and "fornication." Eating of blood is prohibited in God's Dietary Law. Much of our present-day horrible sex sins have their root in this transgression. Read **God's Key to Health and Happiness**.

The Church in Thyatira
Concluding Chapter 2 of The Revelation

"And unto the angel of the church in Thyatira write; These things saith the Son of God, who hath his eyes like unto a flame of fire, and his feet *are* like fine brass" (V.18).

"Works" is mentioned twice in verse 19. The Holy Spirit is not being repetitious (for lack of editing!) but works was the big thing with the Thyatira Church and Age.

V.20, **"Notwithstanding I have a few things against thee because thou sufferest that woman Jezebel, which calleth herself a prophetess, to teach and to seduce my servants to commit fornication and to eat things sacrificed unto idols."** In the Thyatira Church-Age, we see the beginning of Mary worship, the teaching that ministers should not marry, and the commandment to eat a certain food on a certain day, as the pagan sacrifice-to-idols did. The church receded more and more into paganism, and farther and farther from Torah.[6]

V.22, **"Behold, I will cast her into a bed, and them that commit adultery with her into great tribulation, except they repent of their deeds."** This is the only place in the Bible where the expression, "the great tribulation," occurs.

In verses 26-29, again the personal, private relationship of the individual believer with his Lord, is stressed. This cannot be deprived by others, sometimes not even shared, and is quite apart

---

6   The Hebrew word "Torah" is often translated into English as "Law." However, the literal meaning is "Teaching" – God's manual for the man he created. Torah is the first five books of the Bible, written by Moses.

from the human structure of the church:

V. 24, **"But unto you ... which have not known the depth of Satan, as they speak...."** Religious hierarchy hides much from the "laity."

V. 26, **"And he that overcometh, and keepeth MY works** [His works, not ours] **unto the end, to him will I give power over the nations:**

V. 27, **"And he shall rule them with a rod of iron; as the vessels of a potter shall they be broken to shivers: even as I received of my Father.**

V. 28, **"And I will give him the morning star."**

The overcomers of the church-has-supplanted-Israel doctrine will understand the Kingdom Laws and will know the "Star" of a new day (the Son of David, Star of David).

What are the works spoken of in verse 26? Christ's works. What <u>are</u> they? He hasn't deviated from the Abrahamic Covenant nor the Torah.

V. 29, **"He that hath an ear, let him hear what the Spirit saith unto the churches."** But Christendom, for the most part, is deaf to this truth.

The Church in Sardis
The Revelation, Chapter 3

"... I know thy works, that thou hast a name that thou livest, and art dead" (3:1).

The period of The Reformation in church history corresponds to "Sardis." The church of the reformation era had a name for loving the Jews, but turned against them when they couldn't convert them – therefore:

V. 2, "... I have not found thy works perfect before God.

V. 3, "Remember therefore how thou hast received and heard ... If therefore thou shalt not WATCH, I will come on thee as a thief, and thou shalt not know what hour I will come upon thee."

Watch what? – Isaiah spoke clearly of watchmen. *"I have set watchmen upon thy walls, O Jerusalem, which shall never hold their peace day nor night: ye that make mention of the Lord, keep not silence, And give him no rest, till he establish, and till he make Jerusalem a praise in the earth"* (Isaiah 62:6-7).

Notice in Verse 3 they had failed to remember their roots and therefore failed as "watchmen on the walls."

Yet there were real saints among them:

V. 4, "Thou hast a few names even in Sardis which have not defiled their garments; and they shall walk with me in white: for they are worthy."

And again the personal call and promise:

V. 5, "He that overcometh, the same shall be clothed in white raiment; and I will not blot out his name out of the book of life, but I will confess his name before my Father,

and before His angels.

V. 6, **"He that hath an ear, let him hear what the Spirit saith unto the churches."**

When this same admonition occurs at the close of each message to the churches, it's importance is momentous.

The Church in Philadelphia
The Revelation, Chapter 3 continued

"... These things saith he that is holy, he that is true, he that HATH THE KEY OF DAVID...." (V. 7).

In the Philadelphian Church Age the truth of Israel as God's chosen people began to be restored. **"The Key of David"** opens the Scripture and Christ, the Judge of all, deals with destructive, supplanting, replacement doctrine. It is the very Spirit of Messiah, as the son of David that opens, and no man can shut; and shuts and no man can open.

V. 8, **"I know thy works: behold, I have set before thee an open door, and no man can shut it** [including the opening of the continent of America and the establishing of the U.S.A. which has been a base for sending missionaries to pagan lands]: **for thou hast a little strength, and hast kept my Word, and hast not denied my name."**

What is His Name? The God of Israel: the God of Abraham, the God of Isaac and the God of Jacob. *"This is my name forever"* (Exodus 3:15 – This repetition in the Scriptures is for a purpose and it teaches He is a personal God – *"of Abraham, of Isaac, of Jacob"*). The early American settlers recognized the Hebrew Scriptures, as no other Christians had, and named their cities, settlements, etc. with Biblical "Old" Testament names.

The Biblical reference in verse 7 is to the treasurer of the Israeli government under King David. It was he that opened and no man could shut and shut and no man could open. All this refers back to "the key of David" in Isaiah 22:20-24: *"And it shall come to pass in that day, that I will call my servant Eliakim the son of Hilkiah ... And the key of the house of David will I lay upon his shoulder; so he shall open, and none shall shut; and he shall shut, and none shall open. And I will fasten him as a nail in a sure place; and he shall be for a glorious throne to his father's house. And they shall hang upon him all the glory of his father's house...."*

God made Eliakim ruler over the Southern Kingdom *"in the house of David"* and a *symbol* of the true Messiah. God has given the true Messiah of Israel to actually be the key of David that opens and none can shut, and shuts and none can open.

The Apostle Paul preaching in the synagogue at Antioch of Pisidia to his Jewish brethren, reminds them of the Messiah who was to be the key of David: *"... that God raised him up from the dead, no more to return to corruption, he said on this wise, I will give you the sure mercies of David"* (Acts 13:34 – quoting from II Samuel 7; I Chronicles 17; Isaiah 22, etc.) That's solid ground!

Again the problem in the Philadelphian church was remnants of replacement teaching:

V. 9, **"Behold, I will make them of the synagogue** [Greek: assemblage] **of Satan, which say** [profess] **they are Jews** [This is the charge given previously against the church at Smyrna.] **and are not, but do lie** [The Spirit of God charged them with being liars. Here Christ is speaking of all replacement theology teaching, particularlly noticeable in British-Israelism, Anglo-Israelism, etc. We are seeing a revival today under such tags as *Kingdom Now, Dominion, Reconstruction*, etc.]; **behold, I will make them to come and worship before thy feet, and to know that I have loved thee."** Again we say: the overcomer of the church-has-replaced-Israel doctrine understands the Kingdom Keys and knows Him who is the "Morning Star" of that new day.

In the Philadelphian Age, these truths began to be restored. The rebirth of the State of Israel occurred during the latter part of this church age, vindicating those who taught the election of Israel in the Everlasting Abrahamic Covenant.

Verse 9 makes clear that Christ judges those who teach that

the Church has taken the place of Israel and say, "We are the real Jews." This has been the root of anti-Semitism (a more correct term is "Jew-hate") through the centuries. This teaching seeks to cancel out all the promises God made to Abraham and his seed (his family tree through Isaac).

Let us never forget the Abrahamic Covenant is *everlasting*, as clearly outlined in Genesis 12:1-3 and Genesis 17:1-21. We reiterate: Paul confirms this in a few simple words, *"What advantage then hath the Jew and what profit is there in circumcision? MUCH EVERY WAY, chiefly because unto them were committed the oracles of God"* (Romans 3:1 & 2).

Let it be clearly understood: God's sign, token and seal of the everlasting Abrahamic covenant is given in Genesis 17. This blood-shedding token is symbolic of the Pascal Lamb and the True Lamb *"slain from the foundation of the world"* and it all has to do with God's plan of redemption (Romans 2).

At the rebirth of the State of Israel in 1948, and the acquisition of the entire city of Jerusalem and Judea – Samaria (so-called West Bank) in 1967, a minister friend said, *"Replacement teachers lost more theological ground than the Arabs did real estate."* These had to bow to the true messengers of the Philadelphian Church-Age who recognized **"The Key of David."**

But about 40 years later, there was a resurgance of this hackneyed, diabolical teaching, making inroads again into fundamental evangelical churches – even small denominations springing up around these false prophets. But the promise to the faithful and steadfast is:

V. 10, **"Because thou hast kept the word of my patience, I also will keep thee from the hour of temptation** [The "Great Tribulation"], **which shall come upon all the world, to try them that dwell upon the earth."**

The warning of verse 10 is clear: a testing time is breaking, called **"the hour of temptation on all the world"** – but those who have kept the Word of His patience will also be kept by Him in that time.

The purpose of *'The Great Tribulation'* is to show forth the

Glory of the God of Israel. In the following Laodicean Church Age we see that *the tribulation* (judgment) begins with *the House of God* – the purifying of the church and Israel. Will not those who, in a spiritual sense, remain in the Philadelphian Age by keeping His Word and not denying His name, continue to have **"an open door"** and be *kept* during the time of judgment?

Hold On! Faithfully

V. 11, **"Behold, I come quickly** [to bring the Kingdom of God on earth]**: hold that fast which thou hast, that no man take thy crown."**

Don't let go of this restored truth. Your place in the Kingdom when the King returns will depend upon your faithful 'walking in the light as He is in the light.' What are you doing with this truth concerning Israel NOW? This is a wide open door.

Let's get it straight: God is not saving now by nations-full, that is, converting whole nations. Some in America are trying to save the ship of state; others proclaim that they are instruments of God to lead "an army" to save whole nations. But God's invitation to the Gentiles is on a single one-to-one basis, "Whosoever" will may come (John 3:16) – "Whosoever believeth." God has given His messengers responsibility to sow the seed of His Word; it is the work of the Holy Spirit to woo and draw sinful men and women to the Redeemer.

V. 12, **"Him that overcome will I make a pillar** [symbolic of strength and stability] **in the temple of my God and he shall go no more out** [will stay faithful]**: And I will write upon him the name of my God** [that is, His attributes will be seen in him]**, and the name of the city of my God *which is* new Jerusalem, which cometh down out of heaven from my God: and I will write upon him my new name."**

All through the centuries even during hundreds of years of exile, many nations have conquered and occupied Jerusalem, but not one of these have ever had Jerusalem as its capital. It was given to Israel in the beginning and as far as God and all His records are concerned, it has been, and will ever be, Israel's capital. Even during the lengthy and powerful rule of Rome, though controlling Jerusalem as its chief city in the area, Rome's capital was at Caesarea. Recall when Paul appealed his case to Rome, they took him to Caesarea for his trial. The important thing in those days for any land was to have a good seaport. Because Rome ruled the seas in that part of the world, she had to have a good sea base and bastion city for operation and protection in the eastern Mediterranean. Hence: Caesarea.

Jerusalem, of course, is destined to be the center of the world again when Messiah returns. In *The Revelation* (3:12) Christ is speaking of the new Jerusalem which **"cometh down out of heaven from my God."**

We'll learn more about this wonderful 'city' when we get to chapter 21 of *The Revelation*. We shall see later how the names of all the tribes of Israel are written over the gates of this city. This speaks of all the children of Israel and their glorious future.

Hear it Again

V. 13, **"He that hath AN EAR, let him HEAR what the SPIRIT saith unto the CHURCHES."**

The Laodecean Church
The Revelation, Chapter 3 continued

"... These things saith the Amen...."

Verse 14 reveals who Christ really is: **"And unto the angel of the church of the Laodiceans write; These things saith the Amen** [the root is Hebrew for "truth"]**, the faithful and true witness, the beginning of the creation of God."**

The last church era spoken of by Christ is the one in which we now live – the Laodicean Age.

Christ introduces Himself to this church as: **"the Amen** [so be it]**, the faithful and the true witness."** THAT'S WHO HE IS! Think of it! And we can depend totally on HIS WORD.

Then He calls Himself, **"the beginning of the creation of God."** Though Christ is the beginning of Creation, after that God created all things through Christ, as Paul writes: *"All things were created BY HIM and for Him: And He is before all things and BY HIM all things consist"* (Colossians 1:16,17). And note verse 18: *"And he is the head of the body, the Church: who is the beginning* [that is, Christ] *THE FIRSTBORN* [of every creature – and therefore the firstborn] *from the dead.* [Why?] *That in all things He might have the pre-eminence."*

God gives His Anointed One preeminence and requires that we do likewise.

The Apostle Paul – to whom more depth of truth was revealed than any of the apostles or early disciples of the Church – makes it clear. Speaking of Christ, Paul records, *"In whom we have redemption through His blood, even the forgiveness of sins. Who is the image of the invisible God, the first born of every creature* [every created thing]*"* (Colossians 1:14, 15).

It is significant that the "golden text of the Bible" (John 3:16) has this tremendous fact right at its center. *"God so loved the world that He gave His only begotten Son* [BORN-OF-HIM SON] *that whosoever believeth in him shall not perish but have everlasting life."*

God gave His Spirit without measure to Christ (John 3:34; Colossians 2:9): before He ascended unto the Father He said, *"All power is GIVEN unto me."*

As Jesus said to the Samaritan woman at the well, *"God, is a Spirit and they that worship Him must worship Him in spirit and in truth* [God's Word]*"* – also God's two agents by which He has created and performed all things.

Now, Paul in Colossians 1:15 states that Christ – *"is the image of the invisible God."* And since He is in God's image, He also is Spirit, though in order to show what God had done **"before the foundation of the world,"** He came as the **"Lamb of God"** to die (Revelation 13:8). 2000 years ago, God gave Him a body to demonstrate this in a physical form; Christ, speaking to the Father states, *"A body hast thou prepared me"* (Hebrews 10:5).

Peter confirms the same in speaking of the *"lamb without blemish and without spot. Who verily was foreordained BEFORE THE FOUNDATION OF THE WORLD but was manifest* [made known physically] *in these last times for you"* (I Peter 1:19-20).

Paul confirms this to his spiritual son, Timothy: *"God has not given us the spirit of fear, but of power, and of love, and of a sound mind.... Who hath saved us, and called us with a holy calling, not according to our works but according to His own purpose and grace, WHICH WAS GIVEN US IN CHRIST JESUS BEFORE THE WORLD BEGAN. BUT IS NOW MADE MANIFEST* [physically visible] *by the appearing of our Savior Jesus Christ who hath abolished death, and hath brought life and immortality to light through the Gospel"* (II Timothy 1:7, 9 & 10).

In our day, the revival of the unscriptural teaching that the

Church is going to bring the Kingdom on Earth has riveted latent anti-Jewishness which is on the way to becoming a big "wave." Let us not forget that the purpose of the Church Age has been to *"visit the Gentiles and to take out of them a people for His Name"* (Acts 15:14). The Church counsel in Jerusalem fully understood this. Do we think ourselves wiser than the apostles who walked with the Lord in the days of His flesh?

His rejection by his brethren was also according to prophecy, *"God had given them the spirit of slumber; eyes they should not see; ears they should not hear to this day."* Remember – Paul also tells us this "blindness is in part" – i.e., regarding Jesus as Messiah. They are still God's people and are not in total darkness as the pagan world (Romans 11). More on this when we get to chapter 10 of this treatise.

Christ in this letter to the last of all the seven church ages calls Himself, **"the beginning of the creation of God"** and He has more rebuke, reprimand and more criticism of this present church-age than all the others put together. He states:

V. 15, **"I KNOW THY WORKS, that thou art neither cold nor hot: I would thou wert cold or hot."** Many today are coasting along on their own laurels – the "accomplishments" of the Philadelphian Age – and don't even know they are backslidden. They are lukewarm and indifferent toward Israel or else befriend them only as objects of conversion.

V. 16, **"So then because thou are lukewarm, and neither cold nor hot, I will spue thee out of my mouth."**

A cold drink is refreshing; a hot drink is stimulating – but a lukewarm one...? How will He spue it out? In Judgment. When the Almighty brought chastisement upon His people Israel, He said to Jeremiah, *"Though Moses and Samuel stood before me, yet my mind could not be toward this people: cast them out of my sight, and let them go forth.*

"And it shall come to pass, if they say unto thee, Whither shall we go forth? then thou shalt tell them, Thus saith the LORD; Such as are for death, to death; and such as are for the sword, to the sword; and such as are for the famine, to the

famine; and such as are for the captivity, to the captivity" (Jeremiah 15:1-2). In corporal judgment, the righteous also suffer; but as Daniel experienced, God will be with them to strengthen and deliver.

The Apostle Paul reminds us this is an example and we are to be admonished by what happened to Israel (I Corinthians 10:11).

"I" – "I" – THE BIG "I"

The churches congratulate themselves today for the big crowds, for the big beautiful buildings, decorated sanctuaries, wonderful music, rewarding each other with "angels" and "doves." Why does it all make Him sick?

V. 17, **"Because thou SAYEST, I am rich, and increased with goods, and have need of nothing; and knowest not that thou art wretched, and miserable, and poor, and blind and naked."** How could it be any worse? The number of "ands" in this verse serves to emphasize each condition of the Laodecean church. The Spirit of God does not waste words – nor break man's grammar rules without reason.

How and why are we 'wretched, miserable, poor, blind and naked?' Without doubt the greatest offense is our disregard for God's righteous and Holy Law which we've shoved off into a corner called, "Jewish laws."

Now, we're not speaking here about receiving everlasting life by keeping the Law. There is not one passage in either the New or Old Testament that indicates God's gift of eternal life was *ever* by keeping the law perfectly. Still the Law of God is the total substance and description of the complete righteousness of God.

Paul writes, *"by the Law is the knowledge of sin"* (Romans 3:20). Without it we would not know what transgression is. Again Paul writes, *"I had not known sin* [transgression] *but by the law"* (Romans 7:7). Eternal salvation and redemption has always been by God's total grace. And more than that, as Paul writes, *"He has chosen us in him before the foundation of the world"* (Ephesians 1:4). You can't put a fence around that!

Charles Haddon Spurgeon of London, called "the prince of preachers" in his day, stated, *"No man is going to heaven by his works, but it is also true, no man is going to heaven without works."*

The Apostle Paul quotes from Jeremiah 31 concerning this new covenant, *"This is the covenant I will make with the house of Israel after those days saith the Lord: I will put my laws into their mind, and write them in their hearts; and I will be to them a God and they shall be to me a people"* (Hebrews 8:10). He repeats this in Hebrews 10:16 and adds: *"And their sins and iniquities will I remember no more"* (verse 17).

This cannot be said of the Laodicean Church. We have twisted the Law of God into an evil thing. We have misinterpreted Paul's writing, such as in Romans 7 when he speaks of our human nature as *"the law of sin and death."* We have confused the law of sin and death (which is innate in us because of the "fall of man") with God's Law! Paul goes through this thoroughly in Romans 7.

Then in chapter 8 he speaks of the imputed righteousness of God through Christ by faith.

V. 2, *"The law of the Spirit of life in Christ Jesus hath a made me free from the law of sin and death."*

The twisting of Scriptures to make the law of sin and death to be the righteous law of God has done terrible injustice and misleading distortion to the Word of God.

As Paul declares in Romans 8:2 it is the incoming of the Spirit of Life in Christ that brings freedom from the evil nature and its power over us – not "freedom" from God's holy righteous Law.

This misunderstanding and teaching has wrought havoc in the Church and is a travesty against God Almighty.

What has been the result?

First of all, a weak and anemic church that preaches and talks mostly of a Christ who was misunderstood, rejected and finally seemingly defeated and nailed to a cross. It is spoken of and portrayed in passion plays as "a tragedy." That has been the Sunday sermon, for the most part of 51 weeks of every year. On the 52nd, the resurrection is finally proclaimed.

And certainly we need to declare His death, but He declared of Himself, *"No man taketh my life from me. I lay it down of myself"* (John 10:18).

Why?

Because we transgressed God's Holy Law. It was for this reason the Almighty sent forth His Son in the likeness of man and for mankind, condemned sin and transgression and paid the debt.

The giant of the New Testament Church, the Apostle Paul, declared clearly the purpose of Christ's coming and its glorious result:

"There is therefore now no condemnation to them which are Christ Jesus who walk not after the flesh but after the Spirit. For the law of the Spirit of life in Christ Jesus hath make me free from the law of sin and death. For what the law could not do, in that is was weak through the flesh, God sending his own Son in the likeness of sinful flesh and for sin, condemned sin in the flesh:" (Romans 8:1-3).

The greatest act of redemption, the reason of it and the final most glorious result is: *"That the righteousness of the law might be fulfilled in us, who walk not after the flesh, but after the Spirit"* (Romans 8:4).

But the Church has over-emphasized Christ's suffering, His bleeding on the cross, His ridicule by the people. Millions during the centuries have Him still hanging on the cross. And the emphasis has been against Christ's own brethren, the Jewish people who have been dubbed "Christ-killers."

This terrible imbalance of emphasizing His death and not His resurrection has produced devastating results.

To name a few

(1) Terrible bloody Crusades swept down through the Rhine Valley, sweeping away everything in their path, destroying the Jews, burning their villages, filling their synagogues with Jews, then setting them on fire, and cutting down with the sword any who sought to escape. All their properties were confiscated and stolen.

There was the mark of the cross on the garments of these crusaders as they swept toward Israel's holy city of Jerusalem.

Seven times this happened.

(2) Then there was the Spanish Inquistion. I wrote my thesis on it at Bethel Institute, Academy and Seminary at St. Paul. It is too horrible to even give the account, such as the hollowed out, spike-infested, iron maiden into which Jews were put and then it was cranked shut until the spikes pierced the flesh, the face, the eyes. All done in the name of the Church in vengeance for the crucifixion!

(3) And in our generation, the Holocaust of holocausts when the Nazis attempted to annihilate the Jews. This was Germany, the home of the Reformation, "the Bible-belt," so to speak, of Europe!

And what would have happened to the Gentile nations of the world if Christ had not come? if He had not suffered? Christ came with the principle purpose to bear the sins of the world in His own body on the cross and to die for us. And it was for our sins – the Gentile pagan nations of the world, who lay in absolute superstition, fear and mythology without God and without hope in the world.

God chose Israel as a kingdom of priests to all the nations through whom we have been blessed. The type and figures and symbols are laid down in the Hebrew Scriptures. Every tribe had a priest. They would bring the lamb and slay the lamb outside the camp. The body was laid on the altar. Its blood was taken by the priest into the Holy Place. On Yom Kippur, The Day of Atonement, the High Priest would take the blood of the lamb into the Holy of Holies and sprinkle it upon the Ark of the Covenant, making atonement for the entire nation.

Would the tribes of Israel then begin to persecute that godly priest – who was carrying out his duties according to the Scriptures in order that his people in symbolic form would know that their sins were atoned for and that they could enjoy a real sense of peace and forgiveness? Would they then turn against that priest and begin to malign him and say, "You wicked creature. How dare you take the life of that innocent little animal?"

It is a hard thing. But God is showing what our sins do against others; that our transgressions of His Law bring misery and even death to the innocent.

Don't forget it: God did choose Israel as a kingdom of priests as He relates in Exodus 19:5 & 6. And they have been from that time to this. Every ray of divine light and knowledge of God that has ever pierced the darkness of this pagan world has come through the people of Israel.

Suppose God did permit them to be the priests to offer up His Son for the sins of the world, shouldn't we then in thanksgiving for God's mercies praise Him for His plan of redemption?

But don't forget it was Rome that crucified Him. Had the people of Israel performed the execution it would have been by stoning. It was the Roman Government that passed the death sentence upon Him. It was Roman soldiers that put the crown of thorns upon his head and a 'royal' garment upon Him, mocking him as *"King of* [the hated] *Jews."* It was Roman soldiers that crucified him and nailed him to the cross. It was a Roman soldier that pierced His side so that blood and water came out.

Who crucified Him? I and you! The sins of us all.

Yet all who know the Scriptures understand that God is sovereign, and that *He*, in His goodness and grace *"so loved the world, that HE gave His only begotten Son, that whosoever believeth in Him should not perish, but have everlasting life"* (John 3:16).

This subject is of vast importance in studying what Christ **"saith unto the churches"** in *The Revelation.*

The Church in Laodecea – Rejected
The Revelation, Chapter 3 resumed

The "spuing out" indicates the church is in error:

V. 16, **"So then because thou art lukewarm, and neither cold nor hot, I will spue thee out of my mouth."**

Out of what? His mouth! The sin that causes this 'vomit' is the pollution of His Word.

How does He spue it out? By His TWO AGENTS – His Word and His Spirit.

Does God really do this to His own people? Read Jeremiah 15:1. There even comes a point when intercessory prayer is not encouraged by His Spirit.

Why?

"He that turneth away his ear from hearing the Law, even his prayer shall be an abomination" (Proverbs 28:9).

Sometimes these even claim to be "Word" people, but are hearers and not doers. A companion Scripture from the First Testament is Leviticus 20:22, *"Ye shall therefore keep all my statutes, and all my judgments, and do them: that the land, whither I bring you to dwell therein, spue you not out."*

The Revelation chapter 3 and verse 17 again: **"Because thou sayest, I am rich, and increased with goods and have need of nothing"** – materially and spiritually smug.

Covetousness is the root cause of all tribulation. The 10th commandment is the capstone[7] to the others and strikes at the root of all transgression. It was the cause of Israel's captivity and

---

7   Get our *Capstone Commandment* e-book. It is part of our Biblical Insights series available only at the Amazon Kindle Store.

Judah's becoming slaves to Babylon (Jeremiah 8:10).

And it is now the undoing of the Church.

Quote the Word to the Laodicean Church and they will spout it back (or with) you, but are blind to obeying it. **"I know what's in that Word,"** they'll say. **"I don't need you to tell me!"** But the very fact one makes such a remark shows he is not really into the Word, for the more we are, the more we realize we don't know it all! **"... and knowest not that thou art wretched, and miserable, and poor and blind and naked."**

What to DO About it?

His call to counsel is clear here in *The Revelation* as in Isaiah 55:1 *"Ho, everyone that thirsteth, come ye to the waters ... come and buy ... without money and without price."*

Before leaving the rebuke of this present Laodicean church and age, Christ gives some very pointed and specific instructions lest they come before His judgment in utter disgrace, terribly rebuked and severely judged in the great and final day.

Revelation 3:18, **"I counsel thee to buy of me gold tried in the fire."** What is the gold, spiritually? Psalm 19:7-10 gives the clear answer:

"The law of the Lord is perfect, converting the soul: the testimony of the Lord is sure, making wise the simple.

"The statutes of the Lord are right, rejoicing the heart: the commandment of the Lord is pure, enlightening the eyes.

"The fear of the Lord is clean, enduring for ever: the judgments of the Lord are true and righteous altogether.

"More to be desired are they than gold, yea, than much fine gold: sweeter also than honey and the honeycomb." What a promise and truth!

What has been most tried? When we have missed this CENTRAL TRUTH, we have impoverished ourselves!

V. 18 con't., **"and white raiment, that thou mayest be clothed,** [with righteousness – we've already discussed what and how] **and that the shame of thy nakedness do not ap-**

pear; and anoint thine <u>eyes</u> with eyesalve that thou mayest see" – and understand the "mystery" Paul wrote about and the *true doctrine of Christ*. II John 9: ***"Whosoever transgresseth and abideth not in the <u>doctrine of Christ, hath not God....</u>"***
What is the doctrine of Christ? He came manifesting the Father to the world by doing His (God's) Torah-will. He came to fulfill, i.e., to accomplish, to activate the life-giving, happiness-producing Law of God – "walked out" in genuine, unselfish love. This is the "doctrine" (the teaching) of Christ. Let us remember Paul's admonition ***"Let this mind be in you which was also in Christ Jesus"*** (Philippians 2:5-11).

In ancient times when one's sanity was questioned in court, the judge would determine the case by offering the defendant a choice of two objects: a beautiful shiny red-ripe, polished apple and a small gold nugget.

One's spiritual sanity can still be determined the same way. The choice is still between "the apple" – selfish, seducing things and pleasures – and, like Adam and Eve, many today chose "the apple" instead of the gold – The Book of books. King David was spiritually sane in speaking of the Law of the Lord and His precepts, "they are more to be desired than gold, yea, than much fine gold." Which do we take?

Story of Gold

Early in my ministry, we were in evangelistic meetings at a Baptist church in Colorado. We were asked if we would be interested in going to Cripple Creek, Colorado, on Saturday (which was our rest day) and visit a gold mine. We all answered in the affirmative. To make a long story short, we learned something none of us will ever forget. After taking the tour through the mine, and returning near the entrance, they handed us gold bricks to hold. These bricks were valued at that time, approximately $30,000 each. That was back in 1930! Today that gold brick would be worth more like $180,000.

Then they told us this true story

An old mountaineer and his wife had lived in this barren, rugged and stony area many years. He eeked out an existence hunting and fishing in various streams and waters, growing a few chickens, mountain goats, etc.

One day, a stranger came that way and engaged him in conversation as he sat on the small porch of his house. In the course of the visit, the stranger asked the old man, "Have you ever thought of selling this place?"

"No," he said, "not really. Not unless I could get a pretty good price for it."

They continued to discuss the possibility. The stranger said, "How would $200 sound to you?" The mountaineer did not want to seem too anxious so he said, "Well, I'd have to think a lot about that." Continuing, "You might come back in a week or so and I'll give you my answer."

After the stranger left, the old mountaineer went inside and said to his wife, "Do you know this stranger offered me $200 for this old place? The fool doesn't know it's nothing but rocks and wasteland and that he can't grow a thing on it. I didn't want to act too excited. I'm sure going to take him up on it when he comes back."

When the stranger returned a week later, the old men said, relunctly, "Well, we have decided we would sell it for the price you offered." So he did.

The old man and his wife moved down in the valley and bought a little place (which he could in that day for that money) at the edge of the small town. Not long afterward, the stranger brought in a crew with drills. They sank a shaft and soon discovered the richest vein of gold in all the North American continent. He became a multi-millionaire and made Cripple Creek famous for it's gold.

What was the tragedy of the whole affair? The old mountaineer was a millionaire all the time but he didn't know it!

True Gold – Untold!

The Cripple Creek Goldmine is nothing to be compared to the riches, the wisdom and the knowledge of God. The Word of God is full of eternal Truth and instructions which bring glorious living hope made real and vital by the very Spirit of God's in-breathing. His true everlasting "gold" gives not only the promise of eternal life, but peace, joy, guidance, supply and the song of the Lord in the heart – plus health, strength, prosperity and true success. All this is promised of God to the nations of the world through the true Redeemer and Messiah.

Our hearts weep when we think of so many Christians who live as paupers when they could be enjoying the riches God offers so freely in His Word. And not only does this give "the good life" now, but the obedient lay up treasures for all eternity.

Everyone who has the Book of God but rejects or neglects its riches is like the old man at Cripple Creek – a millionaire all the time, but he didn't know it. How tragic!

This is not just a little fairy tale, but an absolute reality. Yet even at that, it is like trying to compare a candle to the shining of the noonday sun to compare the value of gold metal to the immeasurable and unsearchable depth of wisdom, knowledge and understanding in the Word of God. Above all, is the glorious reality that its riches and value can be "mined" by the instrumentality God has given us: His Spirit who applies these life-giving, joy-producing, health-insuring and eternal life promises through Christ.

Christ at the Door

Christ's call to the Laodicean age is:

(1) to be filled with His Spirit and the understanding of His Word that spiritual eyes may be opened;

(2) to forsake materialism for true riches and righteous clothing.

And to accomplish this

V. 19, **"As many as I love I <u>rebuke</u> and <u>chasten</u>; be zealous therefore, and <u>repent</u>."** This is the message.

V. 20, **"Behold, I stand at the door, and knock: if any man hear my voice, and open the door, I will come in to <u>him</u>, and will sup with <u>him</u>, and he with me."**

Verse 20 shows the sad spectacle of this age. Christ is standing outside the door of His Church. His people are in there singing praises to Him, empty though they be. They are boldly declaring His plan of redemption and eternal salvation. They go out and talk about Him then spend the rest of their time and substance on selfish pursuits. They really believe they are part of the inner circle. So in this 20th closing verse, He gives the final invitation: **"If any man hear my voice and open the door, I will come into him and will sup with him and he with me."** This He does by His nourishing Word and the infilling and indwelling of His Spirit.

The call to individuals

(1) hear the invitation of His Spirit and (2) "eat" the Truth with Him. *Learn* the "doctrine of Christ":

And the result of this "open door policy"?

V. 21, **"To him that overcometh will I grant to <u>sit with me</u> in my throne, even as I also overcame, and am set down with my Father in His throne."**

V. 22, **"He that hath an ear, let him hear what the Spirit saith unto the churches."** — Consider God's Golden Key to all these riches which can never fail.

It is Christ who is saying to this present day Church: 'You think you're better than any other people or age? You do not know you're a miserable wretch, poor in heaven's kingdom. Eternally redeemed to everlasting life by the blood of the Lamb of God, yet a pauper throughout all eternity.'

Read what Paul writes in II Corinthians 5:1-11: *"We shall*

appear before the judgment seat of Christ to receive the things done in the body whether it be GOOD OR BAD. Knowing therefore the terror of the Lord, we persuade men." To be a true servant of God, I must drive these things home to our hearts. Christians are going to receive a tremendous shock when they die and come suddenly into the glory world of God the Almighty and all His heavenly hosts.

This is not a judgment as to whether we *enter* the Glory World or not – that has been purchased by Christ *alone* for us – but it will be a judgment of our *position* in that heavenly Kingdom and determine our eternal status in the Kingdom.

Thrones of Glory

The Revelation Chapters 4 & 5

V. 2, "... and, behold, a throne was set in heaven [Highest Authority], and *one* sat on the throne.

V. 3, "And he that sat was to look upon like a jasper and a sardine stone: and there was a rainbow round about the throne, in sight like unto an emerald." This is God the Father Almighty who has never left His throne (Verses. 8 & 9).

V. 4, "And round about the throne were four and twenty seats [thrones] and upon the thrones I saw four and twenty elders sitting, clothed in white raiment and they had on their heads crowns of gold."

The first 12 represent the 12 tribes of Israel, the so-called "Old Testament Saints." The second 12 are the twelve apostles that represent the Church. These are the top 24 rulers in the coming Kingdom of God on earth. They are clothed in white raiment which represents Messiah's perfect righteousness which covers them.

V. 10, "The four and twenty elders fall down before Him that sat on the throne, and worship Him that liveth for ever and ever, and cast their crowns before the throne [Their crowns represent their ruling authority and power which they know is given to them of God] saying,

V. 11, "Thou art worthy, O LORD, to receive glory and honor and power: for thou hast created all things and for thy pleasure they are and were created."

Chapter 5 of The Revelation

V. 1, John the Beloved Apostle and penman of this book writes, **"And I saw in the right hand of Him that sat on the throne** [the throne of God the Father Almighty] **a book written within and on the backside, sealed with seven seals"** – showing its divine authoritative stamp of approval – totally complete, sealed with the seven seals. It is significant that on the backbone of well-bound Bibles, there are seven little raised like bars from top to bottom which represent these seven seals.

"It is Written"

May I drive this home? throughout the New Testament we read the little phrase, *"As it is written"* which refers to a specific place in the Old Testament regarding a similar word symbol, sign, figure, etc.

It bears repeating here that John gave us the secret in the very first chapter and the first verse. In order to preserve the manuscripts he was sending to the various churches, especially in Asia Minor and other places, he told them he was writing this book in "code." They must have a knowledge of the Old Testament Scriptures in order to decipher and break this code in which he was writing.

Remember now especially as we come into the "seals" that the language is symbolic. For instance, when he speaks of "dragon," it isn't actually an earth monster of some kind, but rather satanic powers upon the earth, even some godless governments.

When he spoke of the "stars" of the heaven, he was referring to what God showed Abraham in Genesis 15: God took Abraham out under the stars, told him to look up and said, *"So shall thy seed be."* Therefore, when John spoke of the stars, he was speaking of the people of Israel. And sometimes it has a second application to true believing Gentiles, as Paul wrote, *"If ye be Christ's then are ye Abraham's seed and heirs according to the promise"* (Galatians 3:29).

When John spoke of the "sun" he was speaking about the revelation of the light, the glory and the knowledge of God – some of which is so bright it almost puts out our intellectual eyes. One such blazing light is the over-ruling sovereignty of God in all things.

This is the only way that *The Revelation* can be properly de-coded and its signs and symbols understood.

Christ also used this method of teaching for He spoke in parables. In fact, it was said of Christ, ***"Without a parable He spoke not unto them."***

When John spoke of a "dove," he spoke of the Holy Spirit of God. Also sometimes as the water of life. He spoke of the Spirit of God also as "air" and "wind;" the Hebrew word for both is *"Ruach."*

No doubt the officials of the various nations and countries where the Book John wrote was received, thought, *"This fellow John, has just gone off his rocker, being alone out there on the Isle of Patmos. So he can't be sending any dangerous messages."* It was all "gobbledygook" to them.

Keeping this in mind can help the serious Bible student to read the Book through more knowledgeably. In this volume we seek to consider only our theme, *Israel in the Revelation*.

V. 2, "And I saw a strong angel proclaiming with a loud voice, Who is worthy to open the book and to loose the seals thereof?" – that is, to explain and clearly interpret the Truths that are in the Book of God.

V. 3, "And no man in heaven nor in earth, neither under the earth, was able to open the book, neither to look thereon.

V. 4, "And I [John] wept much, because no man was found worthy to open and to read the book, neither to look thereon.

V. 5, "And one of the elders [no doubt of Israel] **saith unto me, Weep not: behold, the Lion of the tribe of Juda, the Root of David, hath prevailed to open the book, and to loose the seven seals thereof"** – that they may be clearly and fully understood.

"The root of David"

David was the greatest of all the kings of Israel and Israel is the greatest of all the nations upon the face of the earth. All other nations shall eventually come to an end, but Israel has been ordained of God to endure forever, as we shall see as we continue through the Book of *The Revelation.*

It is the true Messiah, the Lion of the Tribe of Judah who opens the seals. The lion, is the king of all the living creatures in the world. The Lord God is giving us an illustration as to whom He has appointed over all the human family: **"The Lion of the Tribe of Judah."** None can conquer this **"Lion"** for his strength and ability overcame all.

Going Back For Facts

What is the origin of **"the Lion of the Tribe of JUDAH?"** We need to brush up on some history at this point, in order to more fully understand THE LION OF THE TRIBE OF JUDAH.

God's whole plan of redemption goes back to Abraham with whom He made an everlasting Covenant (Genesis 12:1-3). The last promise of the golden seven was, *"In thee* [Abraham] *shall all the nations of the earth be blessed."* We have already seen this, and that Paul the chief apostle of the New Testament stated, *"Abraham is the father of us all"* (spiritually – i.e., in things eternal and enduring).

Abraham had a son called Isaac. Isaac had a son, Jacob. Jacob had 12 sons out of which have come 12 tribes of Israel. Rueben was the first-born. According to the law of inheritance, he was the eldest brother who was to be respected as the head of the other 11. His tribe should have been the head, also, of all the other 11 tribes.

However, Reuben fell. He "sold out for" a bowl of (sex) pottage. *"Reuben went* [to his father's own 'bed'] *and lay with Bilhah* [Rachel's handmaid] *his Father's concubine"* (Genesis 35:22). Because of this he was demoted and *Judah* was chosen to head the tribes.

This little bit of further history: During the time Joseph was prime minister of Egypt, a famine was taking place in the land of Israel. You may recall how Joseph held Benjamin for a ransom. (Read the story Genesis 39 to 50.)

Rueben, the first-born, had made a promise to his father, Jacob, explaining, *"The Prime Minister of Egypt said we could get no more grain or food unless we bring our youngest brother, Benjamin."*

But Jacob was adamant. He was *not* going to lose another son of Rachel's – Benjamin – like he had lost Joseph.

Then Reuben used all the persuasive power and influence he had, *"Kill my two sons if I do not bring back Benjamin and the grain."*

But Jacob refused until *Judah* spoke up and said, *"Send the lad with me that we may live and not die. I will be surety for him. At my hand thou wilt require him."*

Father Jacob had total confidence in Judah. It is recorded in Genesis 43. From that day, God had His hand in a very special way on the tribe of Judah, making it a Messianic line through which Messiah should come.

Ordinarily the tribe of the first-born, Reuben, should have been the one to lead the great throng of five to seven million out of Egyptian slavery. But because of Reuben's failure, it was the Tribe of Judah that led all Israel through the 40-year journey.

Tragically, many fathers and husbands have "sold" their right as the true head of their home, forfeiting the respect of the wife and children – all for a new sexual experience – chasing a pot of gold at the end of the rainbow – temporary excitement that blows the home to bits, leaving a broken-hearted mother and weeping children.

If we have strayed from our subject, it is because practical applications need to be made as we go through the Book of God, that have to do with all the various vicissitudes of life.

And so we have it recorded in Revelation 5:5, **"Weep not: behold, the Lion of the Tribe of Judah, the Root of David,**

hath prevailed to open the Book; and to loose the seven seals thereof" – to explain and give its meanings and to give hope unto all the people.

Lion or Lamb? Which? – Both!

The outstanding truth of Revelation 5 is that **"the Lion of the tribe of Judah, the Root of David"** has all authority over the Kingdom which He represents, and He is also presented as the Lamb slain from the foundation of the earth. He alone has the wisdom and knowledge to rightly break the seals – to reveal the meaning of these types, shadows and figures. We need to keep in mind constantly that the Key to *The Revelation* is the 1st verse of the 1st chapter: "sign-i-fied," i.e., in symbols. The Book of *The Revelation* can only be understood in this manner. This is why we repeat this again.

In closing the fifth chapter, we read in verses 11 and 13, that the angels, the living creatures, the 24 elders (Israel and the Church), plus multiplied thousands honor the Lamb of God with seven of the greatest tributes:

V. 12, **"Saying with a loud voice, Worthy is the Lamb that was slain to receive [1] power, and [2] riches, and [3] wisdom, and [4] strength, and [5] honour, and [6] glory, and [7] blessing.**

V. 13, **"And every creature which is in heaven, and on the earth, and under the earth, and such as are in the sea, and all that are in them, heard I saying, Blessing, and honour, and glory, and power, be unto him that sitteth upon the throne** [God the Father]**, and unto the Lamb** [God's Son] **for ever and ever.**

V. 14, **"And the four beasts said, Amen. And the four and twenty elders fell down and worshipped him that liveth for ever and ever."**

This ends the fifth chapter, and corresponds to I Corinthians 15:24-28:

"Then cometh the end, when he shall have delivered up

the kingdom to God, even the Father; when he shall have put down all rule and all authority and power.

"For he [The Executive Director] *must reign, till he hath put all enemies under his feet.*

"The last enemy that shall be destroyed is death.

"For he hath put all things under his feet. But when He saith all things are put under him, it is manifest that He is excepted, which did put all things under him.

"And when all things shall be subdued unto him, then shall the Son also himself be subject unto him that put all things under him, that God maybe all in all."

For a clearer understanding of "the chain of command," get our book: **God the Father & Christ the Son**.

Unsealed & Revealed
The Revelation, Chapter 6

God's **"Lamb"** – the Lion of Judah and the Root of David – opens the seals. He is the only one who can – as an author has the right. As the Lion, He breaks the seals, properly interprets and understands history and executes judgment.

V. 1, "And I saw when the Lamb opened one of the seals, and I heard, as it were the noise of thunder [announcing rain]**, one of the four beast saying, Come and see."**
The first 8 verses of Revelation 6 has to do with the four horsemen that represent 4 different ages. They recount political periods beginning with the first century, A.D. It marks the beginning of the breaking of the seven seals of the Word of God. And each time, one of the heavenly beings in heaven said to John, **"COME AND SEE."** John then briefly describes what he saw.

We see Messiah in His 2 aspects: the Lamb, and also the Lion of the Tribe of Judah. The first time the Messiah came, He came as the Pascal Lamb to lay down his life for the sins of the world, during which times we see only this aspect of God's purposes and plans of redemption. He continues on in this aspect until His second appearance when He shall came as the mighty Lion of the Tribe of Judah to rule and reign over the whole earth from Jerusalem with His people Israel and the Church (as we have seen represented by the 24 elders: representing the 12 tribes of Israel and the 12 apostles of the Church).

These seals continue to be opened by the Lamb, the Messiah, through Revelation 8 until all the judgments named in that chapter are fulfilled.

But let us return to Revelation 6:9.

The Souls Under the Altar

V. 9, **"And when He** [the Messiah-Pascal Lamb] **had opened the fifth seal, I** [John] **saw under the altar** [of God, the Father Almighty in heaven which shelters] **the souls of them that were slain for THE WORD OF GOD and the testimony** [the judicial evidence] **which they held."** Through whom did God the Eternal give all of His Word? How did the Redeemer of the whole world make His appearance on this planet?

BECAUSE the Creator of heaven and earth made an Everlasting Abrahamic Covenant with Abraham and his seed (his family tree); and BECAUSE the greatest and concluding promise of the 7-fold contract is, *"In thee shall all the nations of the earth be blessed"* – IS WHY when we open the New Testament to Matthew 1:1 we read, *"The book of the generation of Jesus Christ, the son of David, the son of Abraham."* Verses 2 begins the long lineage of the family tree of Abraham, down to the birth of Jesus. THIS IS WHY we read in Hebrew 2:16, *"Christ took not upon him the nature of angels, but he took upon him the seed of Abraham."* He had to be born in the land of Israel and specifically in the invironments of Jerusalem at Bethlehem and of a totally-Jewish mother and with a legal totally-Jewish father. And as Christ said to the woman at the well of Samaria, *"Salvation is of the Jews"* (John 4:22).

Is it any wonder then that all the satanic forces of the world through the ages have persecuted, and more than that, shed the blood of millions of the seed of the people of Israel. The Almighty has not forgotten the double-endemnity insurance clause (by the only One Who can really insure life or anything of real value), which insurance reads of Israel, *"I will bless them that bless thee and curse him that curseth thee"* (Genesis 12:1-3). History has borne this out from the birth of Abraham until now. All those who have cursed Israel, God has cursed. And all those who have blessed Israel, God has blessed. *"Let God be true, but* [rather] *every man a liar"* (Romans 3:1-4).

Taking all Scripture into account and the context of the fifth seal of *The Revelation*, it seems clear that these **"souls under the altar"** – under the protection and shadow of the Lord God Eternal – are those of the people of Israel who have been killed – martyred – through the centuries, and in our day particularly, the 6 million slaughtered by Hitler and the Nazis.

The true story is told of a large crowd of Holocaust victims who were herded into a gas chamber, stripped of all clothes and belongings. One tall dignified Jewish man stood in the middle of the crowd as they were waiting for the poisonous gas to be turned on said, "Have no fear, O Israel, in a short time we will see our Messiah."

Many Jews also have died fighting for their homeland. Is it any wonder they say they wish God would choose someone else a while? Why are they called *"God's chosen people"*? It is no light weight title. Returning to verse 9:

"And for the testimony which they held." This word, "Testimony" is in Greek, *"MARTURIA"* (mar-too-ree-ah) – this is *"the Judicial evidences."* God chose them to be writers of every Word of God. They have been the most careful caretakers and preservers of the Holy Scriptures, especially the Hebrew Scriptures. The discovery of the Qumran Scrolls prove this. These scrolls, 1,000 years older than any known until that time, reveal that the Jewish scribes, under God, had kept the Word of God with extreme accuracy. They have kept a *"judicial evidence"* of God's Divine Word. Because they have given the world its only living hope, **"THE WORD OF GOD,"** satanic forces are against them.

Keep in mind as mentioned in chapter one, that when *The Revelation* was written there was no "New Testament." The only Word of God the early Church had for on to 400 years was the so-called "Old" or First Testament. The New Testament itself was originally penned by these sons of Abraham who believed on Christ. But it was not put together in one book until the first

Pope, Damascus, instructed his secretary, Jerome Eusebius, with other helpers to do so.

Jerome, who translated both testaments into the Latin Vulgate (upon which many later translations relied) had real hatred for the Jews, because "they killed Christ." But what if they had?

(The truth is, they didn't. He was sentenced to death by Rome, nailed to the cross by Roman soldiers who guarded the cross and released the body for burial. Plus: the great truth of the Sovereignty of God in Christ's words: *"Therefore doth my Father love me, because I lay down my life, that I might take it again. No man taketh it from me, but I lay it down of myself. I have power to lay it down, and I have power to take it again. This commandment have I received of my Father"* – John 10:17-18.)

What if Christ had not died? It was prophesied in many Old Testament Scriptures. The world would all still be in pagan darkness. It was back in the first century when God initially revealed the Gospel to the Gentiles through His people Israel. They alone had the Word of God and any relationship with God. Then God withdrew them for the most part from the Church (Romans 11) and the Church became largely a Gentile Church.

Note verse 9 again which pointedly involves Israel who **"were slain for the Word of God and for the testimony which they held."** The Holocaust, The Spanish Inquistion, The Crusades. The bloody trail goes on and on, 2,000 years defamed and slain for *"The Word of God"* (Exodus 19:3-6) and testimony "judicial evidence of Scriptures" – as writers and protectors of God's Word. We need reminding again and again that all of the Word of God, both the Old and New Testament were penned by a son of Abraham, in his family tree of Isaac and Jacob – as God had said, *"In thee shall all nations of the earth be blessed."* The first great blessing is God's Word through Israel.

How THE BOOK was born

They had been molded into a nation in the firey furnace and chaldron of Egypt. God delivered them by the blood of the Pascal Lamb on their door posts and door lintels which was a symbol of the true Lamb, (John tells us in Revelation 13:8) slain before the foundation of the world. This was illustrated when God called Abraham to give his son upon the altar. Abraham's faith was so strong in God, God accepted it as done. Israel didn't have to slay their own sons. God gave them the pascal lamb as a type of the sin offering. God came through the land of Egypt that night and said, *"When I see the blood, I will passover."*

Was it the power of the little lamb's blood? No! That was only a symbol of the true Lamb God sent into the world – and honored with a Name above every name. Israel has never neglected from that day through the years each year to keep the Passover. And those that do, come under the same blessing.

Christ at his last Passover Celebration with his Jewish disciples said as He took the bread, *"This is my body which is broken for you."* And when He took the cup, *"This cup is the New Testament in my blood. This do as oft as ye drink it in remembrance of me."* And we Gentiles have come into the household of Abraham in the last promise of the everlasting Abrahamic Covenant, *"In thee shall all nations of the earth be blessed."* He does not say, *"by* thee."

So this word "testimony" in Greek is *"Judicial evidences"* which they have so carefully guarded and protected. What we must garner here and remember is that when Christ broke this 5th seal, John saw under the altar the souls of those who were slain for the WORD OF GOD.

The *"Lawless One"* hates God's Law and Word. This, without question, is the main reason for anti-Semitism – Jew-hate – and the reason the people of Israel have had to suffer such persecution and hardship, driven from nation to nation, tortured and defamed. We remind again: the worst of all these has been in our own day. The indescribable Holocaust. Their lives cut off whether young, middle aged or old, just because they were born of the seed of Abraham which has given us the "testimony" – the Judical evidence – of the Word of God and Christ Himself, "The Incarnate Word."

There were also multiplied thousands of Gentile Christians who died for their testimony, but the greater number of martyrs of the faith have been 'The Chosen Race'. These are they (Israel) who also cry with broken hearts:

V. 10, **"... How long, O Lord, holy and true, dost thou not <u>judge</u> and <u>avenge</u> our blood on them that dwell on the earth?"** This is not generally the prayer of Christian martyrs who as individuals *'called out from the nations, counted it all joy to suffer shame for His name and counted worthy to suffer for the Kingdom of God'* (Acts 5:41; II Thessalonians 1:5) – they also having experienced and confessed their personal testimony and faith in the Word of God which came through Israel.

Parenthetically

Here we must solemnly warn: those who have committed premeditated murder, whatever the reason, shall came face to face *with the one they murdered* at the judgment seat of God!

They are fools who think they kill only the body. (But even the body will be resurrected.) Being ignorant of the Holy Scriptures, they forget after **"God formed man of the dust of the ground, He breathed in to his nostils the breath of life and man became a LIVING SOUL"** (Genesis 2:7). In physical death we only change our venue, our place of existence.

When man can build a computer that can handle millions of transactions per second, what can we expect of the Almighty Who is the source of all wisdom, knowledge and understanding?

Who knows what the Lord God Almighty may have in store? When the Apostle Paul was *"caught up into paradise"* he saw things that were *"unlawful to be uttered"* – but which may be "released" after this phase of our life on this planet is ended. It is something to keep in mind for it won't be long in coming! And as much as lies in us, we must buy up opportunities, as Paul warns, **"Redeeming the time, knowing the days are evil"** (Ephesians 5:6).

Garments of White

These martyrs under the altar who cried out with a loud voice unto God, **"How long, O Lord"**, received a special wordrobe! – clothed with Messiah's imputed righteousness.

V. 11, **"And white robes were given unto <u>every one of them</u>; and it was said unto them, that they should rest yet for a little season, until their <u>fellowservants also and their brethren, that should be killed as they were, should be fulfilled.</u>"**

So the scapegoat of all the political eras (depicted by the Four Horsemen) – is Israel.

We must keep in mind that *The Revelation* is not always written in consecutive order. Perhaps John the Revelator did this to keep the then enemies of God from inflicting further damage.

This will be more evident as we consider coming passages.

The Sixth Seal

This brings us to Revelation 6:12 when **"The Lion of the Tribe of Judah"** the true Messiah opens this sixth seal.

Don't forget in reading *The Revelation* conditions spoken of are in symbolic language, and that **"The Revelation** [is] **of Christ"** (Revelation 1:1). Christ by His Spirit is the Only One who can open the seals and give proper understanding to the Scriptures.

Verse 12 deals with the time that followed an awful slaying of the righteous, when God brings judgment on the earth:

V. 12, **"And I beheld when he had opened the sixth seal, and, lo, there was a great earthquake; and the sun became black as sackcloth of hair, and the moon became as blood."**

In normal times the Sovereignty of God can be seen in various happenings and in the ordinary vicissitudes of life; but in World War II husbands, sons, sweethearts waiting marriage plans were suddenly cut off. Death, casualties and terrible injuries of various kinds deepened the darkness. Hardly any country and hardly even any family was not effected. Normal life was interrupted by rationing of staple foods and supplies – tires and gasoline, etc. Car pools were organized, several workers using one car. Trucks were shared in hauling products to and from a destination point for loading and delivering of essential merchandise and services.

Hitler came into power in 1933 in Germany by a *coup d'etat*. His intents became visible with *"Kristallnacht"* (a German word meaning "the Night of the Breaking of Glass"). A wave of terror began, such as had never been known. The Nazis broke into all the Jewish shops, banks and other institutions. Jews were carted off in cattle trucks and then freightcars, jammed full and crowded into standing only position. Families were torn apart, wives from husbands, children from parents. Heart-wrenching, literally unbelievable cruelty went on and on.

The descriptive language of Revelation 6:12 is, **"Lo, there was a great earthquake."** It was the darkest time of history. The sun which speaks of righteous rulership, law and order **"became black as sackcloth of hair."** Midnight madness reigned with Hitler's Nazi regime. **"The moon** [type of governments of the earth which should reflect the light of God's righteousness, His "Sun"] **became as blood."**

Adolph Hitler instigated the most bloody war of all history that ended with over 30 million casualties. He began in Europe, taking on one nation after the other. He vowed this was to be the war of all wars when he would rid the entire world of all Jews.

STARS

Now we come to Revelation 6:13, **"And the stars of heaven fell unto earth, even as a fig tree casts her untimely figs when she is shaken of a mighty wind."**

The Hitlers of the world have plans for a nightmarish and terrible storm to destroy Israel through whom God has blessed all the nations.

"The stars of heaven fell." Where do we first read of **"the stars of heaven"**? Again we must find the only proper interpretation by going back into the First Testament. The Apostle Paul clearly tells us the Old Testament was written for our admonition, our learning and our example. Therefore, it is impossible to learn what the New Testament properly teaches without having a true knowledge of the so-called "Old" Testament.

Let's go back to Genesis 15, to after the call of Abraham, verse 1, *"After these things* [the plan of world redemption He had just begun with Abraham] *the Word of the Lord came unto Abram in a vision, saying, Fear not, Abram, I am thy shield and thy reward shall be exceeding great."*

V. 5, *"And He brought him forth abroad and said, Look*

now toward heaven and tell the stars if thou be able to number them. And he said unto him, So shall thy seed be." The Lord clearly indicates here that the stars speak of the people of Israel through whom salvation has come.

The mariners through these thousands of years have had to depend on the stars to guide them across the seas and bring them to their desired haven. Our U.S. astronauts in this very modern day of electronics must depend upon the position and movement of the stars in order to keep them on proper course in their astronautical projects (as do also the Soviet cosmonauts).

So God has given us all the light of His Word through Israel which is as the light of heaven reflecting the light of God through His Word.

It is Written

Parenthetically, this is why Jesus Christ for 30 years did not perform a miracle, nor did He give one line of public teaching until the Spirit of God came upon Him. As He was led by the Spirit in to the wilderness to be tempted of Satan, one thing was upmost in His mind.

Satan attacked with, *"If thou be the Son of God command these stones to be made bread."* If you have been to Israel, you have seen this area which is covered with boulders and rocks and stones and pebbles. Satan knowing Christ had fasted 40 days and 40 nights, tempted him with, "If thou be the Son of God, command these stones to be made bread."

Jesus returned Satan's blow with the only offensive weapon we have – the Word of God. He said, *"IT IS WRITTEN."* Whenever this appears in the 'New' Testament, it refers always back to the 'Old' where we must go for our answers and proper understanding of the New Testament. What was Christ referring to?

Deuteronomy 8:3, *"Man shall not live by bread* [food] *alone, but by every word that cometh out of the mouth of God."* In Hebrew the word is "kal" – "ALL – that comes out of God's mouth." There IS more than His Word. It is God's Spirit, as we read when God created man – Genesis 2:7, *"He breathed into his nostrils the breath of life and man became a living soul."* So it is God's Word and Spirit that come "out of His Mouth," without which we cannot be guided.

Falling of Guiding Stars

The Stars are representatives of the Word and life of God pointing the way. We will be lost in every sense of the word, in every area, in every department of life unless we get constant guidance from these stars God has given us through Israel – the whole Book of God.

In that tremendous storm of World War II, Hitler and the Nazis thought they could extinguish the stars of heaven.

Who knows what great and mighty men of God might have come from that 6,000,000 whom Hitler and the Nazis murdered and will meet face to face in the righteous court of the Maker of men. How many God-fearing educators were in that number? How many great prophets? Brilliant scientists that might have solved many of the problems with which we cope so helplessly today?

Other stars fell also. Here in the USA, reports of the war dead began to come in by hundreds and thousands killed in battle. Elongated small banners with a star in the middle were hung in windows indicating a father, husband, brother, or son had fallen in battle. In some homes there were more than one star on the banner. There was the constant fear that a government messenger would come to inform that a loved one was lost in battle. All were glued to their radios.

But the greatest loss of all were six million of the chosen people – through whom all the Light of God there is in this world has come. The purpose of the Third Reich was to annihilate this entire population of "stars." Not only men and women of all ages but a million precious little children were killed. All suffered such injustices and indignities that, the world at large could not believe the reports!

And there is a revival today of this ostrich head-in-the sand attitude! Some still refuse to believe that such could happen in our "enlightened" day. But proof after proof was uncovered. Among our own personal experiences, we have met and known several of these Jewish survivors who still bear the hateful tattooed number of Hitler's death camps on their arms. One such woman saw all her family perish before her eyes. She was allowed to live only for the hard labor she was able to do "for the cause" – the Third Reich!

"Never Again"

We have hope that such will not happen again, now that Israel has their own land, given of God as an eternal possession.

"And I will give unto thee, and to thy seed after thee, the land wherein thou art a stranger, all the land of Canaan, for an everlasting possession; and I will be their God" (Genesis 17:8).

With this final ingathering the Lord gives promise upon promise there will never again be another exile and scattering of His people Israel. Read Isaiah 30:18-21, chapter 54, especially verses 6-9; 66:8-14; Jeremiah 31:10; 50:17-20, 32-34; Ezekiel 36:8-12; Amos 9:15. Notice especially the last one: *"And I will plant them upon their land, and they shall no more be pulled up out of their land which I have given them, saith the LORD thy God."*

World Center Stage

Israel now is World Center Stage. They are the *"apple of God's eye"* (Deut 32:10; Zech. 2:8). All that God does on the international scene has Israel in view. And the God of the Universe calls Himself *"The God of Israel"* <u>88 times</u>. The greatest is yet to come as we shall see when we continue in Chapter 6 of *The Revelation*.

One result of the years ending with Hitler and Nazis was that every "mountain" came down.

V.14, **"And the heaven departed** [spiritually – remember *The Revelation* is given in signs and symbols. It cannot be taken literally] **as a scroll when it is rolled together; and every mountain and island were moved out of their place."** Mountains are symbolic in Scripture of nations and kingdoms.

During our time, the greatest empire that had ever existed – England (of whom it was said, *"The sun never sets on the British Empire"*) – lost her leadership in the world which she had held for 400 years. Canada, Australia, New Zealand, India and many others seceded from the British Empire, as well as many other nations in Africa. The great British Empire broke up into small developing nations, each having the same voting power in the U.N. as the U.S., England, etc. France, also, lost her foreign holdings, as did Holland. We haven't space to deal at length with these and their anti-Israel acts and overtures.

Isaiah 40 speaks of this and is headed by the command to *"Comfort ye, comfort ye my people, saith your God."*

This is the time when more Christian believers and church organizations as well as 'Christian' America have come to comfort and also bless Israel. This international effort is attested by *The International Christian Embassy of Jerusalem* — which was in the birthing stage during one of our residencies there.

Israel's *"warfare is accomplished, her inquiry is pardoned, for she has received of the Lord's hand double for all her sin"* (Verse 2).

Sovereign Purpose

Consider the two World Wars: the first brought about the revival of the *land* of Israel, and World War II brought about the revival of the *nation* of Israel. At the same time we read:

Isaiah 40:4, *"Every valley shall be exalted, every mountain and hill shall be made low."* "Valleys" are symbolic of small nations. These small nations – "the Third World" – had been pretty much in servitude to the large nations.

Even the smallest nation now has one vote in the U.N. General Assembly and in the Security Council, fulfilling this prophecy. "Mountains and hills" speak of the larger nations and they also have only one vote in the U.N. – though the great powers have a veto.

This is preparing the way for the fulfillment of: *"And the glory of the Lord shall be revealed"* (Isaiah 40:5).

Returning to *The Revelation* 6:14: **"And the heaven departed** [i.e., was moved] **as a scroll when it is rolled together** [Not as closing the scroll, but rolling to another section]**; and every mountain and island were moved out of their places."**

The entire map of the world changed, from that of great powers controlling all the smaller nations to merely island countries, such as Australia, New Zealand, England. These in particular were tremendously effected. They came down from mountain empire to islands separated from its "mother" and **"were moved out of their places."**

This shaking of nations is still going on:

V. 15, **"And the kings of the earth, and the great men, and the rich men, and the chief captains, and the mighty men, and very bondman, and every free man, hid themselves in the dens and in the rocks of the mountains;**

V. 16, **"And said to the mountains and rocks, Fall on us, and hide us from the face of him that sitteth on the throne, and from the wrath of the Lamb:**

V. 17, **"For the great day of his wrath is come; and who shall be able to stand?"**

Great men and rulers realizing the potential of the coming electronic powerful arms and missiles began to hide themselves in dens and rocks of the mountains.

It was no secret that our United States government and Pentagon (that is, the high command of the U.S. army, navy and air force) consolidated all of their forces. The so-called impregnable mountain, Mt. Cheyenne, which was almost totally boulders, was hollowed out into a joint headquarters of all forces. There is electronic gear of every possible magnitude which runs into like-electronic fields around the world and at the control of the fingertips of military forces.

The "super powers" are aware of the devastation and destruction that could result from another war – considering the new possibility of these tremendously powerful missiles that could wipe out whole large cities. Even so, there are those military authorities who believe our headquarters will be able to stand intact in this so-called impregnable mountain – a city of military secrets and highly sophisticated electronic gear that became the electronic eyes and brain of our whole U.S. security system, automatically controlled.

If this should fail there is only one alternative and that is to cast ourselves on the sovereignty of God **"who sitteth on the throne"** whose grace is offered through **"the Lamb"** whom the nations of the earth has greatly spurned.

(Special note)

This ends this chapter – the 6th Chapter of The Revelation where Israel is involved. We will continue with Revelation 7 that reverts back to God's original plan. The expression by John is used throughout The Revelation, "I saw, I heard" etc. And so shall we – both hear and see by God's two Agents, His Spirit and His Word.

"Winds of Judgment"
The Revelation, Chapter 7

V. 1, "**AND after these things I saw four angels standing on the four corners of the earth, holding the four winds of the earth, that the wind should not blow on the earth, nor on the sea, nor on any tree.**" – a combination of nations.

"Winds" speak of judgment. And the number four speaks of the earth, so judgment will come from the four corners of the earth. But before that time another angel ascends from the east having the seal of the living God and cries with a loud voice to the four angels holding the wind:

V. 3, "**Saying, Hurt not the earth, neither the sea, nor the trees, till we have sealed the servants of our God in their foreheads.**" Hurt not the established order.

Then follows the sealing of the 144,000 – 12,000 from the 12 tribes of Israel. More regarding this when we get to chapter 14 of *The Revelation*. Vs. 9-17 give the result of the sealing of the 144,000.

V. 9, "**After this I beheld, and lo, a great multitude, which no man could number, of all nations, and kindreds, and people, and tongues, stood before the throne, and before the Lamb, clothed with white robes, and palms in their hands;**"

V. 10, "**And cried with a loud voice, saying, Salvation to our God which sitteth upon the throne, and unto the Lamb.**"

Note here another group "in white". This one (the called out Gentiles) after and because of the sealing of the 12 tribes of Israel. These, too, are "tribulation saints". Vs 16 tells what tribulation is.

Parenthetically – by the Editor

How is the sealing accomplished? Remembering *The Revelation* is not only written in symbolic language, but also, not necessarily in chronological order.

Here is an interesting thought that needs more study: They were "Sealed" (Paul's words in Romans 11 are translated *"blinded in part"*) *"for our sakes"*. These Torah-observant Jews will not intermarry with the nations. They are therefore multiplied by themselves. 12 x 12 = 144 (still symbolic)! This agrees with Paul's revelation that the "blindness" is for our sakes (Romans 11:12, 25, 28). The 'church' of Gentile believers is depicted in Vs. 9 & 10 (above) and follows the sealing of the 144,000. (I realize this is a radical departure from what is generally believed about "the 144,000 Apostle Pauls who will take the gospel during the Tribulation Period.")

Conversion and Intermarriage

Israel was commanded not to intermarry into other religions or with Gentiles: ***"Neither shalt thou make marriages with them; thy daughter thou shalt not give unto his son, nor his daughter shalt thou take unto thy son, for they will turn away thy son from following me, that they may serve other gods; so will the anger of the Lord be kindled against you and destroy thee suddenly ... for thou art an holy people unto the Lord thy God: the Lord thy God hath chosen thee to be a special people unto himself...."*** (Deuteronomy 7:3, 4, 6). They were warned also of this in the commission God gave Moses. (Read Exodus 34:13-16.)

The great evil that results from Jews converting to other faiths is the mixed marriages to Gentiles that the Eternal One forbids. This was the sin of Israel that Ezra the Scribe confessed to God with bitter weeping and lamentations on his return with a remnant from Babylon to Jerusalem in 536 B.C. (Read carefully Ezra chapters 9 and 10.) It was primarily that:

"They have taken of their daughters for themselves, and for their sons; so that they holy seed have mingled themselves with the people of those lands; yea, the hand of the princes and rulers have been chief in this trespass ... Then were assembled unto me every one that trembled at the words of the God of Israel."

Because of this trespass Ezra cried, *"Oh, my God, I am ashamed and blush to lift up my face to thee, my God, for our iniquities are increased over our head, and our trespass is grown up unto the heavens"* (Ezra 9:2, 4, 6).

"Now, therefore, give not your daughters unto their sons, neither take their daughters unto your sons, nor seek their peace or their wealth forever: that ye may be strong and eat the good of the land, and leave it for an inheritance to your children forever. And after all that is come upon us for our evil deeds, and for our great trespass, seeing that thou our God has punished us less than our iniquities deserve, and hast given us such deliverance as this; should we again break thy command-ments and join in affinity with the people of these abomina-tions? Wouldest not thou be angry with us till thou hadst con-sumed us, so that there should be no remnant nor escaping?" i.e., there would be no Jews left because of intermarriage with Gentiles (Ezra 9:12-14).

At that same time, Nehemiah terribly wrought up over this same matter, took a hard line regarding "conversion" and inter-marriage; *"And their children spake half in the speech of Ash-dod* [at that time inhabited with Philistines] *and could not speak in the Jews' language* [Hebrew]*, but according to the language of each people. And I contended with them, and cursed them and smote certain of them, and plucked off their hair and made them sware by God saying, Ye shall not give your daughters unto their sons nor take their daughters unto your sons or for yourselves"* (Nehemiah 13:24, 25).

Nehemiah then reminded them of Solomon's sins of intermar-riage which ultimately brought about the breaking up of Israel into the southern and northern kingdoms and led to their final captivity.

Now back to *The Revelation*.

Chapters 8 & 9

In these chapters of *The Revelation*, we see more judgment on
Gentile powers, **"those men which have not the seal of God
in their foreheads"** (Revelation 9:4). Whatever it's full impli-
cation may mean, only Israel (144,000) is spared the judgment
of "locusts."

The opening of the seventh seal brings forth the seven trumpets (declarations of judgment) announcing war on sin. The
angel (8:3), Christ/Messiah, offers His **"incense"** [symbolic of
prayer] with the prayers of **"all saints"**. – Who are "saints"? For
millennia we Christians have smugly called the church exclu-
sively the "saints". But Paul declared that we are "fellow-citi-
zens WITH the saints" (Ephesians 2).

The "trumpets" bring forth the judgment the prayers of the
saints (and souls under the altar 6:9 & 10) called for. He who
judges is the Angel who receives the prayers of the saints and
offers His "much incense" – intercession – for them.

Beginning with chapter 8, much of the rest of *The Revelation*
is the trumpet and vial judgments centered in the oil-rich nations
of "Babylon" and spreading worldwide as the forces of evil seek
in vain to annihilate the righteous law of God, and His righteous
Son –The Angel with the Golden Censer.

Though it definitely has to do with *Israel in The Revelation*,
there is too much here for one volume. For now we want to look
particularly at a parenthetical chapter which is very illuminating
to the rest of the Book of *The Revelation*. It is central and pivot-
ing – the key to the rest of the Book.

Satanic forces have twisted this truth in the 'Manual of Anti-Semitism': *"The Protocols of the Elders of Zion."* It's pages drip with filthy lies and though proven to be a fabrication,
Jew-haters continue to revive it.

Though *"The Protocols of the Elders of Zion"* can be called

'The Manual of Anti-Semitism,' the cornerstone of Jew-hate in the Church has been replacement theology which continues to be revived. This comes under many names and in various degrees, not only in off-shoot cults, but in mainline and smaller denominations.

However now, from within our Christian ranks, are many coming forth to cry out against this evil. Truth will all be restored. It cannot be annihilated.

Now let us come directly to the 12th chapter of *The Revelation*.

Sun-Clothed Woman
Chapter 12

Now let us quickly pursue, and come to the cause and conclusion of the present world's greatest problem. On the world's center stage are the land and nation of the people of Israel.

Doctor M.A. Ironside, during his pastorate of the Moody Memorial Church in Chicago (perhaps the greatest evangelical church in the U.S. at the time) gave a series of lectures on *The Revelation*. These were put in a volume. I value my personal copy.

Dr. Ironside says on pages 203 and 204 of his book: "I have read or carefully examined several hundred books purporting to expound *The Revelation*. I have learned to look upon this twelfth chapter as the crucial test in regard to the correct prophetic outline. If the interpreters are wrong as to the woman and the man-child, it necessarily follows that they will be wrong as to many things connected with them."

V.1, "**And there appeared a great wonder** [a shocking scene! when God's Spirit calls something "great", it is! And we should give it our total attention.] **in heaven** [secure; forever settled]**: a woman clothed with the sun** [most powerful light of our world and solar system. The sun, a type of God and His Truth – Psalm 84:11; Revelation 1:16 – is the source of all life and energy. God's means of shedding the Light of the world is Israel[8]]**, the moon under her feet** [the moon is a symbol of

---

8   Related thought-provoking verse is Isaiah 30:26, *"Moreover the light of the moon shall be as the light of the sun, and the light of the sun shall be sevenfold, as the light of seven days, in the day that the LORD bindeth up the breach of his people, and healeth the stroke of their wound."* God's Truth will grow brighter and brighter as Israel is restored.

earth's governments. God's law is the basis of governments that reflect the light of God as explained in Romans 13:1-3. Elected and appointed government officials are called "ministers of God," set up to keep order and to which we must be subject to avoid and subdue anarchy], **and upon her head a crown of twelve stars**" – representing the 12 tribes of Israel. At Messiah's glorious appearance, He will establish Jerusalem as world headquarters with all nations sending representatives to the true and righteous UNITED NATIONS.

V.2, **"And she being with child, cried travailing in birth and pain to be delivered."** Read Abraham's vision in Genesis 15:17, and related passages such as Isaiah 51:16-19.

V.3, **"And there appeared another wonder in heaven; and behold a great red dragon, having seven heads and ten horns, and seven crowns upon his head."** The same description is of the "Beast" in Revelation 13:1 – includes intellectual and military powers through earthly rulers.

V.4, **"And his tail drew the third part of the stars of heaven, and did cast them to the earth: and the dragon stood before the woman which was ready to be delivered, for to devour her child as soon as it was born."**

Since with God there is no past, present or future tense, but one great big, eternal present NOW, He reverts to the long cause of Jew hate: satanic forces of pagan Rome attempted to hinder the birth of Christ, through whom God turned to the Gentile nations in fulfillment of the 7th promise in the everlasting Abrahamic Covenant, *"In Thee* [Abraham] *shall all the nations of the earth be blessed."* Roman King Herod, in his attempt to kill Christ, seized and killed all Jewish children under two years old.

Keep in mind the key to interpreting *The Revelation* is given in signs and symbols. The dragon is a type of Satan, with seven heads wearing seven crowns, and ten horns, symbolic of nations. The dragon's stinger-tail drew down one-third of the stars. We have already discussed some of the meaning of stars: even our astronauts must depend upon the stars to guide their otherwise pathless space trips. The light of the stars is still important to our having accurate time. Man has never been able to manufacture a clock that keeps time as perfectly as do the stars. After so many years in order to stay accurate, Greenwich Mean Time and U.S. Marine Time must reset their timepieces by the stars to stay accurate.

The woman (Israel) clothed with the sun (the light of God), in pain ready to deliver the Messiah, was threatened and accosted by anti-God, satanic forces, symbolized by the dragon who stood ready to devour her child. Pagan Rome ruled at the time of Christ's birth and had "seven heads and ten horns." Rome is surrounded by seven mountains and the Roman Empire was made up of ten nations.

V. 5, **"And she brought forth a man-child who was to rule** [shepherd] **all nations** [Goyim in Hebrew] **with a rod of iron: And her child was caught up unto God and His throne.**

V. 6, **"And the woman** [Israel] **fled into the wilderness** [the nations – a spiritual wilderness of paganism with no spiritual life] **where she hath a place prepared of God that they should feed her there a thousand, two hundred and threescore days."** Many of the chosen seed finally found refuge in America, which was a literal wilderness, all through the centuries until the past 200 plus years. This gave them some hope in the beginning, but now it is a great spiritual wilderness, with much profession of faith in God, but idolatrous in many ways.

V. 7, **"And there was war in heaven: Michael** [Michael is the archangel over Israel – as in Daniel 12:1] **and his angels fought against the dragon; and the dragon fought and his angels,"**

V. 8, **"And prevailed not: neither was there place found anymore in heaven.**

V. 9, **"And the great dragon was cast out, that old serpent, called the devil and Satan, which deceiveth the whole world: he was cast out into the earth and his angels were cast out with him.**

V. 10, **"And I heard a loud voice saying in heaven, Now is come salvation, and strength, and the kingdom of our God,**

**and the power of his Christ: for the accuser of our brethren
is cast down, which accused them before our God day and
night."**

The heavenly activity is Michael fighting Satan's attack
against Israel (the woman), who has been accused through the
centuries. It is Christ's brethren, Israel, whom Satan opposes,
and **"accuses them before our God day and night."** Why is
this onslaught against Israel? Note what occurs "in heaven" –
11:19 through 12:7. Satan is cast out of the real Temple area in
the heavenlies, so he vents all his anger on the earthly model!

Satan attacked Israel in the very beginning through Egypt,
making them slaves under the lash of the taskmasters. How
were they freed? The blood of the Paschal Lamb on the doorpost
and door lintels freed them. To reiterate: it was not power in the
blood of an earthly animal, but the blood was a symbol of the
Lamb slain before the foundation of the world (Revelation 3:8).
Israel's deliverance from Egyptian bondage and slavery is the
greatest type of world redemption and the greatest experience in
all Israel's history. They were commanded by God to keep it as a
memorial forever to all generations. Every time Israel celebrates
the Passover, they acknowledge their Redeemer, as God promised, *"When I see the blood, I will pass over you."*

Though we cannot think or grasp all that these terms imply
with our finite minds, yet we can bask in the glorious light of
their peace, joy and confidence which His Spirit gives through
the Redeemer.

But as tragic as it is, "the institutional church", on the whole,
has joined the ungodly in becoming an **"accuser of our brethren."** More than that, the institutional church has invaded the
Hebrew Scriptures at the sordid expense of casting Israel out of
their own house at the whim of us former wicked heathen.

The Almighty warns against cursing Israel, the woman
clothed with the sun, through whom God has given all the light
and spiritual life there is on this planet. Through her has come
all of God's Word and the true Redeemer for all the nations of
the world.

History has proven the Eternal was not just crying, "Wolf! Wolf!" But He carried out these warnings and judgments, from Egypt to Hitler and the Nazis: *"I will undo all that afflict thee"* (Zephaniah 3:19).

God is no respector of persons, but He is a respector of His covenants and He has promised, *"I will bless them that bless thee and curse him that curseth thee"* (Genesis12:3). The purpose of His awesome curse is to protect the people He has chosen to give the whole world His Word and the Redeemer.

To sum up

Since Israel is the chosen vessel in God's hand through whom the Eternal has poured such divine knowledge, light and life – therefore the satanic forces of this world have made Israel their chief target.

V.13, **"And when the dragon saw that he was cast unto the earth, he persecuted the woman which brought forth the manchild."**

Having lost the battle with Michael, Israel's archangel, Satan intensifies his persecution of Israel on Planet Earth. This is not to be taken lightly, and make no mistake about it: no person is a match for Satan's 6,000 years' experience.

Notice the dragon's (Satan) first action: since he could not destroy the Word of God penned by Israel, nor destroy Christ given through Israel Who had ascended unto heaven, Satan then directed all this fury and wrath against Israel who is divinely destined to *"rule* ["shepherd" in the Greek] *all nations from Jerusalem."*

What can be expected in the true Messiah's rule on earth? Here is a partial list of the outstanding measures the Messiah will fulfill and enact:

(1) *"The earth shall be filled with the knowledge of the glory of the Lord, as the waters cover the sea"* (Habakkuk 2:14). See also Isaiah 11:9.

(2) *'Every man will sit under his own vine and fig tree and*

none shall make him afraid' (Micah 4:4).

(3) *'The lion and lamb shall lie down together and a little child shall lead them and play on the serpent's nest'* (Isaiah 11:6 & 8; 65:25).

In the meantime, the battle between "the Sons of Light and the Sons of Darkness" will continue. And the most prominent of all, as we read in Revelation 12:13, satanic forces will continue their onslaught against Israel. But why?

Since Satan cannot pull the Messiah from His heavenly throne, he does everything in the earth he can to continue his battle against the woman (Israel) who brought Him forth as the world's Redeemer.

V.14, **"And to the woman were given two wings of a great eagle, that she might fly into the wilderness, into her place, where she is nourished for a time, and times, and half a time, from the face of the serpent."**

In retrospect, the wings of a great eagle to assist Israel is the U.S.A. (the eagle is the U.S.'s emblem). Over and again when both the U.N. General Assembly and the Security Council, with most every nation, have turned against Israel, she was spared by the power of the U.S. veto.

The Land of Israel, **"her place,"** has also been a **"wilderness"** the past 2,000 years, devastated and destroyed again and again. God provided two wings of a great eagle, to protect from the face of the serpent who, all through history, has tried to destroy **"the woman"** – as all Israel's enemies are now plotting, foolishly. But now it appears the great eagle's wings are being cropped – Why? because we're not faithful to God's Word regarding Israel, but have been unduly influenced by "oil."

V.15, **"And the serpent cast out of his mouth water as a flood after the woman, that he might cause her to be carried away of the flood."**

"Water" is symbolic here of the highly sophisticated false propaganda that Israel's enemies are spewing out of their mouths in outright lies and deception to drown Israel. Much of this propaganda is so wild that it is ridiculous to accept it as credible. But millions of oil dollars behind it puts blinders on many, including some officials in Washington.

However, GOD calls Himself, **"The God of Israel"** – more than any other name throughout the Scriptures. When Moses asked God what he should reply when the Egyptians and the children of Israel asked him who had sent him, God said unto Moses, *"I AM THAT I AM* [You can't put a fence around that] *and He said, Thus shalt thou say unto the children of Israel, I AM hath sent me unto you. And God said moreover unto Moses, Thus shalt thou say unto the children of Israel, The Lord God of your fathers, the God of Abraham, the God of Isaac, and the God of Jacob, hath sent me unto you; THIS IS MY NAME FOR EVER, and this is my memorial unto ALL GENERATIONS"* (Exodus 3:13-15). – Can't put a fence around this either!

"And thou shalt say unto Pharaoh, Thus saith the LORD, Israel is my son, even my first-born: And I say unto thee, Let my son go, that he may serve me: and if thou refuse to let him go, behold, I will slay thy son, even thy first-born" (Exodus 4:22, 23).

God sees all Israel as an entity, "His son." He deals and makes His covenant of salvation with *"the House of Israel and the House of Judah"* (Jeremiah 31:31).

There is no "whosoever" in God's dealing with Israel, as when He turned to the pagan Gentile world. At the biggest church business meeting in the New Testament "the whole church" discussed *"what miracles and wonders God had wrought among the Gentiles"* and Simeon (Peter) declared how *"God at the first* [i.e., the First occasion. Peter was referring to the time he was sent to the house of Cornelius, a Gentile.] *did visit the Gentiles, to take out of them a people for His Name"* (Acts 15:14).

The Apostle James goes on to quote Amos 9:11 & 12, *"After this* [i.e., after the Gentile Church Age, at which we are now nearing the end] *I* [the true Messiah of Israel] *will return, and will build again the tabernacle of David, which is fallen down; and I will build again the ruins thereof, and I will set it up:*

"That the residue of men might seek after the Lord, and all the Gentiles, upon whom my name is called, saith the Lord, who doeth all these things" (Acts 15:16 & 17).

And here is the Rock to hook your anchor to:

"Known unto God are all his works from the beginning of the world.

"Wherefore my sentence is that we trouble not them, which from among the Gentiles are turned to God: But that we write unto them, that they abstain from (1) *pollutions of idols* [materialism – idolatrous pollution]*, and from fornication* [sexual uncleanness, rampant where God's family-preserving Laws are violated] *and from things strangled, and from blood* [dietary laws].

"For Moses of old time hath in every city them that preach him, [teaching right from wrong] *being read in the synagogues every Sabbath day"* (Acts 15:18-21).

This was written especially to the Gentile Church, but the Church, for the most part, has not heeded the admonitions.

Coming back to *The Revelation* Chapter 12:

V. 16, **"And the earth helped the woman, and earth opened her mouth, and swallowed up the flood which the dragon cast out of his mouth."**

God has set up some true friends of Israel, who are not in the crowd of those who huckster them with lies that they are children of Satan bound for hell. We have in our files some of this propaganda that says, *"Send us your dollars to keep Jews from tumbling into hell."* – Selling souls on the slave market. God has made promise, make no mistake about it, *"I will curse them that curseth thee."* These are God's chosen people with whom He has made an *Everlasting* Covenant.

Again we reiterate: The phrase, *"God is no respector of persons"* is true as to the color of skin or money in the bank, but GOD IS A VERY CAREFUL RESPECTOR OF HIS COVENANTS. *"I know that whatsoever God does, it shall be forever: nothing can be put to it, nor anything taken from it: and God doth it that men should fear before him"* (Ecclesiastes 3:14).

And *"I am the Lord, I change not"* (Malachi 3:6).

In Conclusion

One part of the ministry of Bible Light International is to *help* literally swallow up, i.e., neutralize and defuse all these lies against Israel, theologically and otherwise – above all by the command of God Himself: *"Comfort ye, comfort ye my people, saith your God. Speak ye comfortably to Jerusalem, and cry unto her, her welfare is accomplished, her iniquity is pardoned: for she hath received of the Lord's hand double for all her sins"* (Isaiah 40:1,2). Read the rest of this chapter in the Book of Isaiah to see the mighty God of Israel. He promises to track down to the last man any who dare lay a false report on His people. In a plural way God blesses: *"I will bless __THEM__ that bless thee,"* but to the last man: *"I will curse HIM that curse thee"* now. Not one will escape.

The cemetery is not the end of the road – it's just the beginning of the longest existence. Foolish people feel they can violate any of God's laws and get by. No one does! A murderer thinks he has wiped out a man for eternity – just by pulling a trigger. How foolish. Every premeditating murderer *will come face to face* with the one whose life he cut short on earth. He will have to look him straight in the eye. *"It is appointed unto men once to die* [it has been true so far] *but after this the judgment"* (Hebrews 9:27).

In the 6th chapter we saw those who were murdered asking God to avenge them. This seems to be the victims of Holocausts, Inc.

"Life is real, life is earnest and the grave is not the goal.
"'Dust to dust and ashes to ashes' was not spoken of the soul."

We urge all who read this to *join that* number yet on earth who help the woman (Israel). We – us of the nations – owe them a great debt for being the instrument of *His Word* and the true Redeemer whose face shines brighter than the noonday sun. Israel suffers for our salvation's sake. How dare we condemn her?

The dragon continues to attempt to destroy Israel **"who keep the <u>commandments of God</u>"** – which many in the Church twist to their own undoing. It is Israel, also, who has the **"Judicial evidences"** – true records of Messiah.

Beastly Blasphemy
The Revelation, Chapter 13

The Word of God has many facets. As a jewel shaped in the hands of the craftsman has many facets which catch light rays bringing out the beauty of the stone, so God's Word brings light and beauty, understanding and strength to meet the believer's personal and present need.

In reading to understand such portions of Scriptures as the seemingly difficult symbols of *The Revelation*, let us not get bogged down in and restricted to the interpretation Mr. Know-it-all has been preaching. Let us come *'boldly to the throne of grace and obtain mercy and grace to help in time of need.'* If we need interpretation of a certain passage, we have the promise of the Spirit of Truth to lead into all Truth.

In this 13th Chapter of *The Revelation*, we see two "beasts" coming up out of the "sea." "Beasts" is generally symbolic of world systems, and "seas" represent the nations.

That there will be, in the near future, a *"beast"* known as the anti-Christ, is generally accepted among evangelical Christians. However, in this study, let us lay aside for the time the idea of the "anti-Christ" being one particular being – person, ruler – and consider the culture that produces such a "Frankenstein."

Blasphemy

V. 1, **"And I stood upon the sand of the sea, and saw a beast rise up out of the sea, having seven heads and ten horns, and upon his horns ten crowns, and upon his heads the name of**

blasphemy."

"For as he thinketh in his heart, so is he" (Proverbs 23:7).

The dictionary defines blasphemy as *profanity, mocking, denying the existence or providence of God.*

Since the Garden of Eden when Satan made the tempting suggestion "You shall be as God," mankind has attempted to replace God. Instead of considering God to be sovereign, our great "educational" systems for the most part enthrone "the free will of man" and encourage the "SELF image."

A classic example of educational failure is the great universities of Berlin. In the midst of this, Hitler was listening to satanic blasphemy against God's chosen race and sought to destroy them. Was not he and his Nazi regime a "beast"?

V. 7, **"And it was given unto him to make war with the saints, and to overcome them: and power was given him over all kindred, and tongues, and nations."** Did Hitler not wage war against the "saints" – God's chose people – and overcome them? Others besides Jews were his victims, but the Hebrew race was *singularly* targeted.

Did not this beast have power to bring the nations into World War II? It is interesting to note that our U.S.A. was in the war 3½ years (see verse 5). And did not Hitler and Germany receive a "deadly wound?" Yet the whole world witnessed the crash of the Berlin wall in '89 – and now a resurfacing of Jew-hate and neo-Nazism, and not only in Germany!

We ask the question: Is the 2nd beast of Revelation 13 rising up from the sea to resurrect the old blasphemous system? What today is the greatest of anti-Christ and anti-Israel systems?

His "mark" received in the forehead speaks of <u>mind control</u>; the mark in the right hand speaks of world economy.

The Apostle John said, *"the whole world lieth in wickedness"* (I John 5:19).

Harvest Time
The Revelation, Chapter 14

V. 1, **"And I looked, and lo, a Lamb stood on the mount Sion, and with him an hundred forty and four thousand, having his Father's name written in their foreheads."**

What people have **"the Father's name written in their foreheads [minds]"**? Those "sealed" in Chapter Seven; by the first fruit of redemption (verse 5).

This calls to mind the words of the angel Gabriel to Mary, *"Thou shalt call his name Jesus for he shall save his people from their sins."* Did he fail? No! A thousand times "NO."

The Apostle Paul tells us, also, He came to *"confirm the promises made unto the fathers: AND that the Gentiles might glorify God for His MERCY"* (Matthew 1:21; Romans 15:8,9).

What a debt we owe. Because Israel is sealed in the Everlasting Abrahamic Covenant we have the gospel preached **"unto them that dwell on the earth...to every nation...."** (V. 6). The results of the gospel in the 2,000-year church age are recorded in *The Revelation* 7:9 & 10.

This will finally bring down "Babylon" – the evil trinity of idolatry: the seat of the devil, the flesh and the world's system.

The "seal" of the 144,000 which is the "Father's name written in their foreheads" is the direct opposite of the "mark of the beast" (V. 9).

V. 12, **"Here is the patience of the saints: here are they that keep the commandments of God, and the faith of Jesus."**
What is the faith of Jesus? He has not changed faith – He came to confirm it as we read a minute ago, AND He came to teach

the WORLD the will of the Father – *"The God of Israel."* The Anointed One's job will be accomplished – Let us come along with Him!

V. 18, **"And another angel came out from the altar** [where the souls "under the altar" prayed for righteous judgment, Revelation 6:9]**, which had power over fire; and cried with a loud cry to him that had the sharp sickle, saying, Thrust in thy sharp sickle, and gather the clusters of the vine of the earth; for her grapes are fully ripe.**

V. 19, **"And the angel thrust in his sickle into the earth, and gathered the vine of the earth, and cast it into the great winepress of the wrath of God.**

V. 20, **"And the winepress was trodden without the city, and blood came out of the winepress, even unto the horse bridles, by the space of a thousand and six hundred furlongs."**

We reiterate: in addition to failing to remember that *The Revelation* is written in "signs and symbols," is the error of expecting all these events to be in chronological order. God operates in Eternity – without limit of time.

Israel, the vine (Ezekiel 15) *was crushed* in 70 A.D. The destruction of Jerusalem began God's record-keeping for the nations treatment of His scattered "vineyard" these 2,000 years. Will God not judge the religious of the earth for their treatment of His people Israel since that time?

Then follows the great judgments of the plagues and vials of Chapters 15-18 which is also a subject for another volume! Sufficient here is to say the chief culprit is personified in "Babylon" – and the call to God's people (Israel and the believers from the nations) is to **"come out of her, my people, that ye be not partakers of her sins, and that ye receive not of her plagues. For her sins have reached unto heaven, and God hath remembered her iniquities"** (18:4,5).

How is this "coming out" accomplished?

By *teshuvah* (Hebrew for return, repentance) filling the mind and heart with God's Word and making it our 'life-style' which is accomplished by yielding to His Spirit, the great Revealer of

His Word (John 16:13).

Now let us come quickly to the final chapters of the Book of *The Revelation* and see how the Lord wraps it up!

The Coming New World Order
The Revelation Chapters 21 & 22

The consummation of the old order and the beginning of the new is spoken of in *The Revelation* as **"The New Jerusalem"** coming from heaven **"prepared as a bride for her husband"** (every condition ideal – Revelation 21:2).

Why "Jerusalem"? Because:

"The Law [Torah – teaching] *shall go forth of Zion and The word of the LORD from Jerusalem"* (Micah 4:2 and Isaiah 2:3).

V. 10, **"And he carried me away in the spirit to a great and high mountain, and showed me that great city, the holy Jerusalem, descending out of heaven from God,**

V. 11, **"Having the glory of God: and her light was like unto a stone most precious, even like a jasper stone, clear as crystal;**

V. 12, **"And had a wall great and high, and had twelve gates, and at the gates twelve angels, and names written thereon, which are the names of the twelve tribes of the children of Israel:**

V. 13, **"On the east three gates; on the north three gates; on the south three gates; and on the west three gates."** Compare Ezekiel 48:30-35 which gives the names of the Tribes on each of the four sides.

V. 14, **"And the wall of the city had twelve foundations, and in them the names of the twelve apostles of the Lamb."**

What was foundational Truth the Apostles of Christ taught? It was The Gospel – The "Good News" of deliverance from a life of sin, and the power through Christ to **"overcome"** and to

"walk in white" (Revelation 3:5). In Him [Christ] Grace and Law blend beautifully.

Jerusalem, the new golden city John envisioned will be established as God's eternal capital. God will honor His people Israel, the instrument in His hand through which salvation has come to all the earth, by engraving the names of the twelve tribes over the twelve colossal gates of the new Eternal City of Jerusalem.

This means that no one has greater proof that their names are written in heaven than Israel. The Spirit of God specifies, not the names of the "twelve (men) patriarchs" but (all the people of) the "twelve tribes."

The Lord God omnipotent, not only thus identifies Himself with the people of Israel throughout all eternity, but assures them a top honored place in heaven.

Would He have the names of the twelve tribes before Him for all the ages upon ages to come if the great vast majority of them were cast out into outer darkness and everlastingly lost?

Are we to believe that Satan could forever boast, *"The Almighty has their names on His gates, but I have His people in my eternal place?"*

May none imply our gracious, loving, compassionate God to be a thousand times worse than a Hitler. He would not give His dazzling everlasting promises of *world redemption* through Israel, dangling it before them with no intention of fulfilling it *to them.* Would this not be like a mother nurturing an unborn babe in her bosom for nine months, day by day looking forward with great anticipation and joy to its arrival, but finally it is taken from her at its birth and given to a stranger, leaving her destitute?

V. 21, **"And the twelve gates were twelve pearls; every several gate was of one pearl: and the street of the city was pure gold, as it were transparent glass."**

"Pearls" are formed by friction from a foreign substance. This has been the saga of the Jewish people for millennia.

V. 25, **"And the gates of it shall not be shut at all by day: for there shall be no night there."**

There will be perfect understanding of Israel's position and role in the Kingdom.

Coming world redemption, peace and prosperity will come through Zion. Therefore:

"For Zion's sake will I not hold my peace, and for Jerusalem's sake I will not rest, until the righteousness *thereof go forth as brightness, and the* salvation *thereof as a lamp that burneth.*

"And they shall call them, The holy people, The redeemed of the Lord: and thou shalt be called, Sought out, A city not forsaken" (Isaiah 62:1, 12. Read the whole chapter.).

Concluding Note

Admittedly, there are many passages that are *"hard to be understood,"* as the Apostle Peter wrote (II Peter 3:16), and Moses declared, *"The secret things belong unto the Lord our God, but those things which ARE revealed belong unto us and to our children forever"* (Deuteronomy 29:29).

The Scripture speaks of the whole subject of Israel's "blinding" to Christ at His first coming as a "mystery"; could we comprehend it fully, it would no longer be a mystery. We must commit it and ourselves unto God *"as unto a faithful Creator."*

And the Book ends with the declaration given by the Hebrew Prophet Isaiah (62:11) which reads, *"Behold, the Lord has proclaimed* unto the end of the world, *Say ye to the daughter of* Zion, *Behold, thy salvation* [Hebrew – "Yeshuah" – Joshua, translated into English, "Jesus"] *cometh; behold his reward is with him and his work before him."* Salvation is spoken of here as a person, "Yeshuah."

Jesus quotes this verse from Isaiah in *The Revelation* 22:12; **"Behold, I come quickly; and my *reward* is with me, to give every man according as his work shall be."** He closes with His signature, in verse 16; **"I, Jesus, have sent mine angel to testify unto you these things in the churches."**

He informs the Church as to His roots, declaring, **"I am the root and the offspring of David** [reminding Gentiles "salvation is of the Jews"] **and the bright and morning star,"** – symbolized by the star (shield) of David, the ***Mogen***.

The Lord promises concerning Himself: ***"I, the Lord, have called thee in righteousness, and will hold thine hand, and will keep thee, and give thee for a covenant of the people, <u>for a light of the Gentiles</u>"*** (Isaiah 42:6).

The entire Book of God, this divine lamp and light unto our feet, was penned by sons of Abraham. It has blessed nations and people with cultural, moral and spiritual light and freedom where it has been received. Where it has been rejected – fear, bondage and superstition, moral and spiritual darkness prevails.

The Redeemer at His first coming, turned primarily to the Gentiles as the **"bright and morning star"**. He is the **"day star"** that has arisen **"in your hearts"** to lighten and brighten the lives of millions of true believers around the world through the ages.

Now when ***'the fulness of the Gentiles is completed'*** (Romans 11:25), The Anointed One will soon return to His own people, Judah who will effectively minister God's Word to the nations. Messiah shall then appear and ***"arise as the Sun of righteousness with healing in His wings"*** for all people, flooding the world with His light, fulfilling all other Messianic promises (Isaiah 11:4-9; Joel 3; Micah 4: Zephaniah 3:8-20; Zechariah 12-14).

Preparations for His coming continues at a feverish pace in Israel, though not known even to some of the builders, as the word of Isaiah, the prophet, admonished, ***"Arise, shine, for thy light is come and the glory of the Lord*** [the pillar of fire – the Shekinah, divine presence that led Israel through the wilderness and that abode in the Holy of Holies of the Tabernacle and Temple; and, above all, that was given without measure to Messiah, John 3:43] ***is risen upon thee"*** (Isaiah 60:1).

After 2,000 years the pendulum is now swinging back to His people Israel from the Christian nations that have had light so long but have turned from it. ***"For behold*** [moral, political and spiritual] ***darkness shall cover the earth, and gross darkness*** *the people* [Gentiles] *but the Lord shall arise upon thee and His glory shall be seen upon thee"* [Israel] – Isaiah 60:2.

And the Lord declared to Israel, *"Not for thy righteousness or for the uprightness of thine heart, dost thou go to possess the land, but for the wickedness of these nations ... and that He may perform the word which the Lord sware unto thy fathers, Abraham, Isaac and Jacob"* (Deuteronomy 9:5).

National Symbols

It is singularly significant that Gentile nations have wild beasts and birds as state symbols: the USA, the eagle; England, the lion; Russia, the bear; China, the dragon, etc. But Israel has the Menorah, the seven golden candlestick, as was ordained for the Temple and symbolic of the light of God. Israel was chosen in the beginning from Abraham's time as *"the burning lamp,"* as the world's light (Genesis 15:17).

Christ, who is of the seed of Abraham, identifies himself with His people, Israel, in *The Revelation* 1:12 as the candlestick (menorah). When God in Christ turned to the pagan world 2000 years ago, Christ became this pagan world's light and declared, *"I am the light of the world; he that followeth me shall not walk in darkness, but have the light of life"* (John 8:12). And He said of His true followers, *"Ye are the light of the world"* (Matthew 5:14).

Since the time of Christ, the true Church has been a candlestick as spoken by the Lord in *The Revelation* 1:12 which has given the light of the binomial (the written and incarnate) Word of God to the pagan nations. And we must never underestimate the power of the gospel of the true Christ of God to transform pagan lives. Neither must we confuse the castigated and deformed Christ taught in Christendom, with the true Messiah of Israel.

Since the fulfillment of Luke 21:24, the retrieving and uniting of Jerusalem, Israel's regathering takes on a much greater significance in the light of Jerusalem becoming the Bible-predicted world capital. God again will make them the light unto the nations as His kingdom of priests, according to His original plan (Exodus 19:6), remarkably indicated now by modern Israel's State symbol, the candlestick.

It is written of them: *"The sun shall be no more thy light by day; neither for brightness shall the moon give light unto thee: but the Lord* [Israel's Redeemer-Messiah] *shall be unto thee an everlasting light, and thy God thy glory.*

"Thy sun shall no more go down; neither shall thy moon withdraw itself; for the Lord shall be thine everlasting light, and the days of thy mourning shall be ended" (Isaiah 60:19, 20).

It is evident, therefore, that if we are to have a knowledgeable concern in the redemption of the nations and world peace, we must be concerned with Israel's welfare, prosperity and blessing.

If Any Thirst

The Messiah at the end time declares, **"I will give unto him that is athirst of the fountain of the water of life freely."** Closing the canon of Divine Scripture the Spirit of God invites, **"And let him that is athirst come, and whosoever will, let him take of the water of life freely"** (Revelation 21:6, 22:17).

The invitation is open.

I must personally witness that it is this living water given of the Lord God of Abraham, Isaac and Jacob through the Redeemer-Messiah that has been my 'satisfying portion' the past sixty years. It ended my pleasure chase.

The people of Israel who suffered torturous thirst in the wilderness found physical fulfillment in drinking water out of the rock at Horeb after Moses had smitten it as God ordered. The people drank and were satisfied; a physical symbol of a spiritual truth. The Rock was a type of the world's Redeemer who was smitten for our transgression. When his side was pierced, there came forth, not only blood for the cleansing of sin so that we *"shall not perish,"* but there also came forth water, a symbol of His resurrection power and Spirit that we might *"have everlast-*

ing life" (John 19:34 and 3:16).

Rock of Ages Insurance

From Galatians 3:15-17 it is very clear that Paul is speaking of the Everlasting Abrahamic Covenant, and Messiah bound up in it with His people.

We read, *"Brethren, I speak after the manner of men; Though it be but a man's covenant* [but this was the Lord God Eternal's covenant] *yet if it be confirmed, no man disannulleth, or addeth thereto...*

"And this I say, that the covenant that was confirmed before of God IN CHRIST...."

Yet some have tried to annul this covenant, robbing God of His divine honor and magnanimous grace to Israel to the terrible risk of God's warning given in *The Revelation* 22:18, 19.

V. 18, **"For I testify unto every man that heareth the words of the prophecy of this book, If any man shall add unto these things, God shall add unto him the plagues that are written in this book:**

V. 19, **"And if any man shall take away from the words of the book of this prophecy, God shall take away his part out of the book of life, and out of the holy city, and from the things which are written in this book."**

Verse 11 shows the distinction between righteousness and evil solidified:

V. 11, **"He that is unjust, let him be unjust still: and he which is filthy, let him be filthy still: and he that is righteous, let him be righteous still: and he that is holy, let him be holy still.**

V. 12, **"And, behold, I come quickly; and my reward is with me, to give every man according as his work shall be."**

The **"root and the offspring of David, the bright and morning star"** is the Prince of this Holy City who declares, **"Surely I will come quickly."**

And our hearts echo **"Even so, come, Lord Jesus"** – *Yeshua*

– salvation – with deliverance of every kind.

   Until that glad day:

   The grace of our Lord – the Savior and the Anointed One be with you all. – Amen.

About the Author

Elmer Axene Josephson was born in Kansas City, Missouri, December 19, 1909, of Swedish (Gentile) immigrant parents. The call of God to the ministry of His Word came at the age of 19.

His public school education was supplemented at Bethel College and Seminary, St. Paul, Minnesota, and at Moody Bible Institute of Chicago. He traveled extensively as an evangelist and held three pastorates. He was ordained in the American Baptist Convention early in his ministry. He chartered and directed the work of Youth for Christ International in Wichita, Kansas in the early 50's.

From the beginning of his ministry he majored in Bible prophecy, reading and studying all he could find on the subject. He married Christine Crawford at Wichita, Kansas January 1, 1961, and they worked together in the Bible Light ministry which has its roots in years of study of the Holy Scriptures and of experience in all various areas that pertain to our Judeo-Christian heritage, and is a challenging influence within the evangelical community to arouse the Christian conscience toward the emerging nation of Israel. He was instrumental in encouraging Christians in the investment of Israel bonds and to bless the nation in Wmany other practical ways. The Josephsons have hosted many tours to Israel and have an aggregate of 8 years residency in Jerusalem and environs.

Rev. Josephson authored many books, including the best-seller published by Bible Light Int'l., "God's Key to Health and Happiness" – which truths added over 60 years to his life. He departed this life October 27, 1996, but his work lives on in the many manuscripts and books which continue to be published.

To find other publications by Bible Light authors, search the Amazon.com website.

What is Bible Light?

Founded by Elmer Josephson in 1956, Bible Light International is classified by the IRS as a non-profit religious organization. It is not a membership-structured organization with 'rules and dues' to promote its own organization worldwide. Bible Light does seek to be that which its name implies, to: **"write the vision and make it plain that he may run who readeth"** (Habakkuk 2:2).

Bible Light is a challenging influence within the evangelical Christian community to arouse Christian conscience toward the nation of Israel and stimulate expressions of encouragement to the Jewish community in its aspirations to restore the Land of Israel.

Bible Light does not seek to be a denominational church nor to compete with churches. **We seek to be an arm of the "invisible Church" outstretched in love toward Israel. We recognize the unique position of God's chosen People in the Everlasting Abrahamic Covenant** (Genesis 12:1-3; 17:1-21).

The Josephsons have an aggregate of ten years' residencies in Israel. We've been publishing since 1957. How do we do it? We have a little motto: **"When He leads, He feeds; when He guides, He provides."** But the promise of having our needs supplied can only be realized as we are faithful stewards of what God puts in our hands.

For additional information, write: **Bible Light International**, PO Box 370, Ottawa, Kansas 66067-0370, or visit our web site: www. Bible-Light.com where you may discover other titles not available through the Amazon.com, or learn of other opportunities enabling you to honor and bless others.

www.ingramcontent.com/pod-product-compliance
Lightning Source LLC
Chambersburg PA
CBHW060808050426
42449CB00008B/1597